REFORMING MERCY MINISTRY

A Practical Guide to Loving Your Neighbor

TED RIVERA

IVP Books

An imprint of InterVarsity Press
Downers Grove, Illinois

InterVarsity Press
P.O. Box 1400, Downers Grove, IL 60515-1426
World Wide Web: www.ivpress.com
Email: email@ivpress.com

InterVarsity Press® is the book-publishing division of InterVarsity Christian Fellowship/USA®, a
movement of students and faculty active on campus at hundreds of universities, colleges and schools of
nursing in the United States of America, and a member movement of the International Fellowship of
Evangelical Students. For information about local and regional activities, write Public Relations Dept.,
InterVarsity Christian Fellowship/USA, 6400 Schroeder Rd., P.O. Box 7895, Madison, WI 53707-7895,
or visit the IVCF website at www.intervarsity.org.

All Scripture quotations, unless otherwise indicated, are taken from THE HOLY BIBLE, NEW
INTERNATIONAL VERSION®, NIV® Copyright © 1973, 1978, 1984 by Biblica, Inc.™ Used by
permission. All rights reserved worldwide.

While all stories in this book are true, some names and identifying information in this book have been
changed to protect the privacy of the individuals involved.

"Give Hospice Care" written by Robin Colby. Used by permission.

Cover design: Cindy Kiple
Interior design: Beth Hagenberg
Images: two boys running: Tom Stoddart/Getty Images
　　　　mother holding son: © webking/iStockphoto
　　　　portrait of a homeless man: © adl21/iStockphoto

ISBN 978-0-8308-4421-0 (print)
ISBN 978-0-8308-9594-6 (digital)

Printed in the United States of America ∞

 As a member of the Green Press Initiative, InterVarsity Press is committed to protecting
the environment and to the responsible use of natural resources. To learn more, visit
greenpressinitiative.org.

Library of Congress Cataloging-in-Publication Data

Rivera, Ted, 1960-
　Reforming mercy ministry : a practical guide to loving your neighbor /
Ted Rivera.
　　pages cm
　Includes bibliographical references.
　ISBN 978-0-8308-4421-0 (pbk. : alk. paper)
　1. Mercy. 2. Compassion—Religious aspects—Christianity. 3. Church
work. I. Title.
　BV4647.M4R58 2014
　241'.4—dc23
                                                              2014013400

P	18	17	16	15	14	13	12	11	10	9	8	7	6	5	4	3	2	1
Y	29	28	27	26	25	24	23	22	21	20	19	18	17	16	15	14		

Contents

Preface

ALL OF US, IN ONE WAY OR ANOTHER, appear in the pages of this book. We are a damaged species; none of us comes to the end of our journey without struggle, without pain—without needing one another.

With this thought in view, we ought to consider it a privilege that we can give of ourselves to others, in specific ways, as others will likely one day give of themselves for us.

Evangelicals quite often fail to connect *serving others* with *sharing the gospel*; they often think of these actions as being entirely distinct from each other, so that to do one means forgoing the other. Other Christians, meanwhile, quite often subsume the latter into the former; they fail to articulate the gospel, assuming that by serving others they've effectively shared their faith.

Helping other humans is not evangelism. Neither, however, is it *in conflict with* evangelism. Rather, serving others is often the soil in which the gospel best flourishes.

In this book I aim to show the proper relationship of *mercy ministry*—a way of referring to the various ways we, motivated by our Christian faith, attend to the needs of others—to the Great Commission, and to help us think more clearly and biblically about the ways we attempt to help one another. A significant backdrop for this work is a well-known but vital passage of Scripture found near the end of the Gospel of Matthew: Jesus' presentation of the sheep and the goats.

When the Son of Man comes in his glory, and all the angels with him, he will sit on his glorious throne. All the nations will be gathered before him, and he will separate the people one from another as a shepherd separates the sheep from the goats. He will put the sheep on his right and the goats on his left.

Then the King will say to those on his right, "Come, you who are blessed by my Father; take your inheritance, the kingdom prepared for you since the creation of the world. For I was hungry and you gave me something to eat, I was thirsty and you gave me something to drink, I was a stranger and you invited me in, I needed clothes and you clothed me, I was sick and you looked after me, I was in prison and you came to visit me."

Then the righteous will answer him, "Lord, when did we see you hungry and feed you, or thirsty and give you something to drink? When did we see you a stranger and invite you in, or needing clothes and clothe you? When did we see you sick or in prison and go to visit you?"

The King will reply, "Truly I tell you, whatever you did for one of the least of these brothers and sisters of mine, you did for me."

Then he will say to those on his left, "Depart from me, you who are cursed, into the eternal fire prepared for the devil and his angels. For I was hungry and you gave me nothing to eat, I was thirsty and you gave me nothing to drink, I was a stranger and you did not invite me in, I needed clothes and you did not clothe me, I was sick and in prison and you did not look after me."

They also will answer, "Lord, when did we see you hungry or thirsty or a stranger or needing clothes or sick or in prison, and did not help you?"

He will reply, "Truly I tell you, whatever you did not do for one of the least of these, you did not do for me."

Then they will go away to eternal punishment, but the righteous to eternal life. (Matthew 25:31-46)

If we were to consider the many activities of the Christian church in sum, we might conclude that this passage has had little influence. And yet the primary preoccupations of Christians—Bible study, daily devotions, evangelism and common worship—are conspicuously absent from Jesus' view of the future judgment in this passage. As important as worship, evangelism, devotion and Bible study may be, in light of this passage our priorities, our activities, and indeed our passions likely must change. We ourselves must dramatically change.

The purpose of this book is to stir us from our comfortable cocoons. The surgeon Ben Carson rightly laments,

In our culture, security . . . dictates everything from public policy to Madison Avenue's commercial appeals, from medical care to education and personal and family life. We buy every kind of insurance—from life insurance to replacement policies for our cell phones—to provide us with the security we think we need.[1]

The teachings of our Lord Jesus are unconcerned with insurance. They function as a clarion call, pulling us out of our comfort and out of our seeming security and safety, and into the messy work of sharing the gospel and serving others.

There is one gospel, but there are surely at least thirty-three ways whereby we can help others—we ourselves, not some designated surrogate or impersonal program. As you consider the thirty-three ways detailed in this book, try to align your heart with the concerns that are presented. Ask yourself, "Could this be my story?"

Introduction

Won't I Be Your Neighbor?

> *Love your neighbor as yourself.*
>
> **LEVITICUS 19:18**

HAVE LIVED A HAUNTINGLY SELFISH, self-consumed, little life. This isn't a confession so much as a bald statement of fact. Maybe you are like me. If so, you're at a crossroads—you have begun to recognize an emptiness in your life, and you've begun to want to do something about it. It's time to begin the journey of compassion.

Christians regularly fret about and plan about and think about a journey of compassion, but few actually go through with it. Compassion is messy. It's rarely fun. Compassion involves deliberate human contact, and humans who need compassion are deeply flawed and so very disappointing. We are never far into the journey of compassion before we are tempted to quit.

The people who lived in the dorm rooms near mine in college were deeply flawed and utterly disappointing to me. Their musical selections and hours of operation rarely met with my approval. And so I avoided most of them.

Later my wife and I moved into a little apartment in North Tarrytown, New York. The neighbors below us cooked noxious-smelling things and yelled grammatically awkward Spanish at one another, while the Iranian neighbors above us sounded even more foreign and enjoyed wrestling with one another each and every night. We definitely avoided all of our neighbors there.

We eventually moved to get away from the cacophony below and the tumult above. Our new landlord's dog was insanely yippy, however, so we avoided our landlord as much as possible. Then we moved to the suburbs.

Sweet glory, all about us. Distant, sanitized neighbors, easily avoided as we moved from one ever more spacious home to another. Now nameless neighbors wave at the right times for the right duration; they never trouble us to borrow gasoline for their riding mowers. Bliss.

All the while, of course, people are living and dying all around us—in America where we live and, more particularly, in far-off lands. In some ways, America is the Majority World's suburb; we are comfortably removed from music and smells and languages and wrestling and yipping animals that make us uncomfortable. Self-indulgence. Self-gratification. Self-reliance. Self-regard. Self-interest. Self-esteem. Self-improvement. Self-absorption. These terms clutter the American lexicon; name another country on the face of the earth better suited to invent a magazine called *Self*. Spend some time traveling and you notice how eager the rest of the world is to learn about what is going on in other countries; by contrast, America is seen as almost wholly insular and self-absorbed—and seems to live up to the reputation. We live during a season in human experience when disengagement is all too common, and the better off you are (and we in the United States are, by and large, well off indeed), the easier disengagement becomes.

Harriet Jacobs was born into slavery in Edenton, North Carolina, and spent the better part of her childhood oblivious to the fact that she was a slave. But she was a slave. Her "mistress," as she called her ("owner," as we might), was a Christian woman; she taught Harriet verses from the Bible. Later, when Jacobs looked back on her childhood experience, she reflected on the disconnect between her mistress's faith and her conscience: "My mistress had taught me the precepts of God's Word: 'Thou shalt love thy neighbor as thyself.' 'Whatsoever ye would that men should do unto you, do ye even so unto them.' But I was her slave, and I suppose she did not recognize me as her neighbor."[1]

Our Christian journey of compassion begins when we remember how to be a neighbor. It's not as easy as it sounds once one gets out of practice. Neighbors can be loud, and disappointing, and smelly, and foreign. Neighbors can be exactly the type of people we long to avoid.

Fortunately, we are not left without guidance. When God became man in the person of Jesus, he was full of stories—one of the ways he broke through the preconceptions and religious shackles of his day. In his story about a good Samaritan, Jesus identified for us a man who truly acted like a neighbor.

In the two thousand years since Jesus looked into the eyes of a Jewish expert in the law and told him about a man who fell into the hands of robbers, this penetrating tale that once shattered racial prejudices and spoke of a better way has lost some of its punch; in the hearing of many, in fact, it begins to sound like nothing more than the clanking of new religious shackles—an antiquated legalism that privileges acts of charity over the grace of God.

Clarence Jordan recognized this problem and sought to help us once again grasp the essence of this parable:

> One day a teacher of an adult Bible class got up and tested him [Jesus] with this question: "Doctor, what does one do to be saved?"

Jesus replied, "What does the Bible say? How do you interpret it?"

The teacher answered, "Love the Lord your God with all your heart and with all your soul and with all your physical strength and with all your mind; and love your neighbor as yourself."

"That is correct," answered Jesus. "Make a habit of this and you'll be saved." But the Sunday school teacher, trying to save face, asked, "But . . . er . . . but . . . just who is my neighbor?"

Then Jesus laid into him and said, "A man was going from Atlanta to Albany and some gangsters held him up. When they had robbed him of his wallet and brand-new suit, they beat him up and drove off in his car, leaving him unconscious on the shoulder of the highway.

"Now it just so happened that a white preacher was going down that same highway. When he saw the fellow, he stepped on the gas and went scooting by.

"Shortly afterwards a white Gospel song leader came down the road, and when he saw what had happened, he too stepped on the gas.

"Then a black man traveling that way came upon the fellow, and what he saw moved him to tears. He stopped and bound up his wounds as best he could, drew some water from his water-jug to wipe away the blood and then laid him on the back seat. He drove on into Albany and took him to the hospital and said to the nurse, 'You all take good care of this white man I found on the highway. Here's the only two dollars I got, but you all keep account of what he owes, and if he can't pay it, I'll settle up with you when I make a pay-day.'

"Now if you had been the man held up by the gangsters, which of these three—the white preacher, the white song leader, or the black man—would you consider to have been your neighbor?"

The teacher of the adult Bible class said, "Why, of course, the nig—I mean, er . . . well, er . . . the one who treated me kindly."

Jesus said, "Well, then, you get going and start living like that!"[2]

Neighbors may look like us, or they may look like all the people we hope we never have to see. You may have gotten past prejudices against white people, for example. Good for you. Or you may have overcome ancient biases against black folk. Well done. Who bothers you now?

- Is it that Mexican, sneaking his way over your border?

- Is it that gringo, holding you back?

- Is it that smelly bum who won't let you get into Starbucks without waving an empty cup in your face?

- Is it that inarticulate secretary of yours? That obnoxious boss?

There are just so many deeply flawed and disappointing souls in our world. They're the people we're called to be neighbors to and who, more often than not, are better neighbors than we are.

James Orbinski, past president of Doctors without Borders, asks a question that is increasingly echoed in the culture we inhabit: "How are we to be in relation to the suffering of others?"[3]

Humanitarianism is about more than medical efficiency or technical competence. In its first moment, in its sacred present, humanitarianism seeks to relieve the immediacy of suffering, and most especially of suffering alone.[4]

Orbinski identifies himself as a Roman Catholic, but his humanitarian work and the organizations he has been a part of have been consciously secular in their orientation. Such organizations pursue the question of how we love our neighbor—often risking their lives in the process—without appeal to the teachings of Jesus.

One wonders why on earth someone—and indeed, why *many* people—would subject themselves to such risk apart from a vibrant Christian faith. But when asked, "Why do you do it?" Orbinski's response was simply "Because we can."[5] It's a Samaritan response to a question that our theologizing often makes more complex than it needs to be. One could imagine Jesus pointing to Orbinski or any number of secular exemplars and telling us, his faithful followers, "Go and do likewise."

Each of the chapters that follow will seek to remind us of things that would make our world a better place. In every case, taking action will be hard, and the way may not be as clear as people might wish it were. But we should do them anyway, "because we can."

Like me, perhaps you want to one day hear Jesus the storyteller tell you, "Well done, good and faithful servant! Come and share your master's happiness!" That seems like a life well lived. But in the meantime we live our lives against the backdrop of the American dream, with its ever more creative ways to be self-indulgent in ever more titillating ways.

Jesus calls us to something different—to share the gospel and serve others. In this we can begin to work on thirty-three ways to cross the road from self-indulgence to Jesus' ministries of mercy. We can learn how better to help others and, in the process, learn to recognize our neighbor. Harriet Jacob's Christian mistress never crossed that road. Perhaps in our case there's still time.

FOR FURTHER REFLECTION

Rewrite the parable of the good Samaritan, incorporating your own prejudices and inner demons. Be unsparingly honest. Read your parables to a group of friends or as part of a class discussion. Or send your story to me at actnow@33ways2help.org.

1

Feed the Hungry

I was hungry and you gave me something to eat.

MATTHEW 25:35

CHRISTIANS HAVE GROWN ADEPT at feeding themselves spiritually, and Western Christians often go for the deluxe plan. We wake up in the morning and, with a piping hot mug of justifiably expensive Bolivian coffee sweetened with just a hint of saccharine, pore carefully over our Bibles with pen or highlighter in hand. Perhaps we keep Oswald Chambers's *My Utmost for His Highest* or Charles Spurgeon's *Faith's Checkbook* or the little booklet *Our Daily Bread* at the ready. We lift little prayers for mama's aches and daddy's bowel, for the situation with the troublemaker at work or, very typically, with respect to our self-induced financial woes.

We make our way to the office, singing along with Christian radio or, craving more edgy contemporary Christian music, with our neatly organized iPods. On Tuesday night we go to Bible study, on Wednesday night we go to prayer meeting (seeking broader intercession for mama's aches and daddy's bowel), and on Sunday we gather with the spiritually "mature" for Sunday school and morning and evening worship. Once a month we make it to a boutique men's or women's study group tailored to our particular felt needs.

And if we're really lucky, we'll have time to blog about it all.

Such is the life truly well spent, the life that pleases God, we will imagine. But is this really what God intends the mature Christian life to look like?

Walk through your typical corporate Christian bookstore, and you will find whole sections on personal growth. But you'll almost never find a section titled "Mercy Ministries." For many Christians "mercy ministry" evokes notions of social justice, which evokes images of dirty hippies worshiping the sun while engaging in subversive social engineering. The "social gospel," as a mashup of gospel truth and social transformation, is for many an oxymoron—the two don't belong together.

If we were to do an audit of the agendas of most Christian churches—or individual Christians, for that matter—feeding people who are hungry wouldn't rank high on the list. (By contrast, it's quite high on the agenda of most hungry people.) Perhaps this has to do with the fact that people who need food aren't particularly influential, and influence is generally perceived to be the coin of the realm in the kingdom of God. Smelly people keep us from drawing larger crowds, and larger crowds smell like success. Sometimes "successful ministries" impede biblical ones.

How did such attitudes come to reflect the Christian life? When did feeding ourselves spiritual confections become the aim of Christian living? By severe contrast, there is a call to utter selflessness in the Bible, a call to absolute self-abnegation and self-forgetfulness, a call not to self-esteem but to *other*-esteem that seems lost in all of our Bible conferences and retreats and podcasts and revivals. Did we overlook the book of Proverbs in all of that Bible study?

- "One man gives freely, yet gains even more; another withholds unduly, but comes to poverty. A generous man will prosper; he who refreshes others will himself be refreshed." (Proverbs 11:24-25)

- "If a man shuts his ears to the cry of the poor, he too will cry out and not be answered." (Proverbs 21:13)

- "A generous man will himself be blessed, for he shares his food with the poor." (Proverbs 22:9)

- "He who gives to the poor will lack nothing, but he who closes his eyes to them receives many curses." (Proverbs 28:27)

The prophet Isaiah declares that the kind of fasting demanded—decreed—by Almighty God is to "share your food with the hungry" (Isaiah 58:7). This is a very different kind of fast than we might have been taught. Consider as one example the influential work of Richard Foster, who speaks of fasting as one of the "inward" spiritual disciplines. Although he considers numerous Scriptures on this topic, Isaiah's command is not among them. "Fasting must forever center on God," he suggests.

> Once the primary purpose is fixed in our hearts, we are at liberty to understand that there are also secondary purposes in fasting. More than any other single Discipline, fasting reveals the things that control us. . . . Fasting helps us keep balance in life. . . . Numerous people have written on the many other values of fasting such as increased effectiveness in intercessory prayer, guidance in decisions, increased concentration, deliverance for those in bondage, physical well-being, revelations, etc.[1]

Isaiah challenges this solitary notion of fasting.

> Is this the kind of fast I have chosen, only a day for a man to humble himself? Is it only for bowing one's head like a reed and for lying on sackcloth and ashes? Is that what you call a fast, a day acceptable to the Lord? (Isaiah 58:5)

Instead, our God through Isaiah pleads with his people to "spend yourselves in behalf of the hungry" (Isaiah 58:10). This implies an exertion, effort, an outward focus, the necessity of looking beyond our own pain and our own situation in order to express practical, ongoing, personal service to others. And the promised reward is profound to the one who heeds this call: "Then your light will rise in the darkness, and your night will become like the noonday" (Isaiah 58:10).

Should we be tempted to ignore Isaiah, James 2:14-17 will sharply rebuke us:

> What good is it, my brothers, if a man claims to have faith but has no deeds? Can such faith save him? Suppose a brother or sister is without clothes and daily food. If one of you says to him, "Go, I wish you well; keep warm and well fed," but does nothing about his physical needs, what good is it? In the same way, faith by itself, if it is not accompanied by action, is dead.

Despite all of our efforts to feed ourselves spiritually, could the reality of our own spiritual hunger be, in part, a symptom of our ignorance or avoidance of these biblical commands?

MEETING THE HUNGRY

Admittedly, a personal involvement with those who experience hunger can be genuinely painful to us, and even potentially dangerous. L. Shannon Jung in his thought-provoking *Hunger and Happiness* speaks with candor about a situation with which perhaps each of us can relate—actual encounters we might routinely have with people in dire circumstances.

> My morning route to Saint Paul School of Theology takes me past a QT gas station. . . . There are any number of derelicts and people who look as though they have slept out in the open or not at all. Often there is an old woman whose shoes have seen much better days. This woman is gray-haired and

wrinkled, and she often wears a worn gray sweatshirt and a nondescript skirt. She usually stands about five feet inside the door, looking as if she does not know where she is and certainly not where she is going.

I'll admit that I don't like seeing this woman, and I try to distance myself from her. . . . My temptation is to run away from this person who exhibits vulnerability and pain.[2]

As good as it is to have organizations caring for hungry people around the world, we are not absolved by the Scriptures from being involved ourselves. The most prosperous communities have people who are struggling on its fringes. As one clear example, consider Westchester County, New York, with a population of just under a million souls. Despite being one of the wealthiest counties in the United States, "the Food Bank for Westchester estimates that approximately 200,000 county residents are hungry or at risk of hunger. More than half of them are seniors; one-third are children under the age of 18."[3] Even if the Food Bank's estimate is greatly exaggerated, we get a sense of how prevalent the problem of hunger might be right in our back yards.

It's certainly true that Jesus said, "The poor you will always have with you" (Matthew 26:11), and that with respect to certain slackers Paul counseled that we not even let them eat (2 Thessalonians 3:6-13). Elsewhere in the Bible, however, we see the other side of the biblical equation—hungry people experiencing God's glorious blessings:

> The poor will eat and be satisfied; they who seek the LORD
> will praise him—may your hearts live forever!
> (Psalm 22:26).

Her poor will I satisfy with food. (Psalm 132:15)

As Haregewoin Teferra learned, in caring for orphans in Africa, "When in doubt, feed first."[4]

FOR FURTHER REFLECTION

This isn't rocket science. Virtually every community has a program or a group that is active in feeding the poor. If yours doesn't, start one!

You will sometimes find it hard to insert yourself into these programs or groups, in large measure because they are stretched too thin to coordinate volunteers effectively. You will often find them administratively challenged. Persevere. Overcome. The best way to be truly effective is to remain committed for a long period of time.

In addition, develop a global concern. Identify groups that are reaching out around the country and around the world to effectively help hungry people, and support them with your dollars and service. Raise awareness within your church about such ministries.

Short-term mission trips are good. Long-term mission trips are better. Go where no one else is willing to go, and be prepared to endure great hardship with little encouragement.

Write down ten ways you can potentially help the hungry over the next year. Pray that God will help you to follow through on the impressions that the Holy Spirit might make upon you by his Word.

2

Fight Famine

Have I not wept for those in trouble?
Has not my soul grieved for the poor?

JOB 30:25

A poor man's field may produce abundant food,
but injustice sweeps it away.

PROVERBS 13:23

THE PROBLEM OF HUNGER is daunting in its own right. Famine is a problem of such scope and complexity as to defy comprehension. When we hear of the dire situation in parts of Africa or in other parts of the world—when we hear about it at all—we often find ourselves unable to effectively process the information. The images we see of bloated and starving children, presented as they sometimes are in appeals for funds or in the rare news account, often compel us to look away or change the channel. "Some viewers," we are warned, "will find aspects of this next story disturbing." Politics and war are common complications that render traditional aid approaches ineffective. And the list of overarching problems goes on and on: natural disasters, severe drought, economic, cultural, ethnic and religious conflicts. By contrast to other problems we're faced with, famine appears to be an intractable problem, one that requires governments and world leaders and denominations to intervene. What could we possibly do on an individual level that would make any kind of worthwhile impact?

Famine is characterized by an utter hopelessness that renders us mute and powerless. But we must somehow speak, and we must somehow act. This will require unusual wisdom.

COMPETING CASES

Imagine that we have entered a courtroom of ideas where two titanic intellects have risen to challenge one another. Even at the outset of this conflict, it will be important for us to remember the ancient words of Proverbs 18:17: "The first to present his case seems right, till another comes forward and questions him."

The first to come forward is none other than the esteemed economist Jeffrey Sachs. In the domain of economics, Sachs is indisputably a rock star, not least because Bono wrote the foreword to his book *The End of Poverty*. The Earth Institute at Columbia University, where Sachs serves as director, avers that Sachs "is widely considered to be the leading international economic advisor of his generation."[1]

For a moment, allow your heart and mind to drink in the magnanimous hope *The End of Poverty* conveys. What if we *could* live in a world free from poverty, from hunger, from famine? Is such a world really possible? Sachs says yes.

> Around the world, people are opening their eyes and hearts to these marvelous possibilities. Schoolchildren, college students, retired professionals, actors and actresses, corporations and foundations, and private foundations, and private philanthropists are all entering the fray. The Live 8 concerts, Bono's

ONE campaign, Angelina Jolie's work for the United Nations, and many other acts of leadership and grace, are drawing millions of eager individuals into a new commitment to work for the end of poverty, and thereby for a world of peace and shared well-being.[2]

Sachs presents dozens of graphs and charts, and a torrent of data, giving us ample reason to listen attentively. When he quotes Ghandi and Kennedy and Martin Luther King Jr., we are inspired. He concludes, "Let the future say of our generation that we sent forth mighty currents of hope, and that we worked together to heal the world."[3]

To speak against such an authority seems not only foolhardy but cold-hearted. Or is it? There is a profound difference between activity and effectiveness, and while we may rightly feel as if we must do *something*, it is far better to do something that will be *effective*.[4] While one cannot question Sachs's sincerity or the worth of his aims, one can question his data, and this is of paramount importance as it relates to the crippling problem of famine.

The other economic titan to weigh in on this topic is William Easterly, whose unnerving thesis is captured well in the subtitle to his book *The White Man's Burden*—"Why the West's Efforts to Aid the Rest Have Done So Much Ill and So Little Good." Easterly speaks of the "legend" that Sachs and others have perpetuated, which can be summarized in this way:

> The poorest countries are in a *poverty trap* (they are poor *only* because they started poor) from which they cannot emerge without an aid-financed *Big Push*, involving investments and actions to address all constraints to development, after which they will have a *takeoff* into self-sustained growth, and aid will no longer be needed.[5]

Easterly aims to debunk this legend and consider approaches that may have a more positive impact. He draws a contrast between the massive plans pulled together by "planners"—bureaucrats who are disconnected from the day-to-day realities of poor countries—and the workable microchanges that can be implemented by those on the ground ("searchers").

Paul Polak, in his book *Out of Poverty,* likewise emphasizes on-the-ground effort over against planner-driven programs: "Most poverty experts spend little or no time talking with and listening to extremely poor people in the places where they live and work. . . . You can't sit in your office at the World Bank or in your research lab at Stanford and figure out what to do about poverty in Myanmar."[6]

One of the many powerful examples of concrete action is the problem of combating intestinal worms. In one region in Kenya, 92 percent of children were infected by these worms, causing "listlessness, malnutrition, and pain."[7] Economists Michael Kremer of Harvard and Edward Miguel of Berkeley discovered that programs that emphasized education on behaviors to prevent worm infection were failing to change the situation.[8] They ultimately devised a "practical scientific approach" to the problem, giving children deworming drugs so they could stay in school.

The point is clear: fighting *famine* is impossible. Fighting intestinal worms in one region in Kenya through proven methods is attainable. Rather than indiscriminately throwing money (even vast sums) at a problem, addressing specific needs for specific communities with those communities' involvement can make a meaningful difference. And yet, notwithstanding their personal sincerity or legitimate concerns, many people continue to fall prey to the high ideals of planners without sufficient regard for local outcomes, as identified by the searchers.[9]

Of course, any efforts we might personally make as Christians to combat famine may encounter the bleating of contemporary Phar-

isees who would chide us with charges of—*horror!*—proclaiming
the social gospel. In his book *Famine in the Land,* Steven Lawson
avers that "*true* preaching, *biblical* preaching, *expository* preaching—
is the greatest need in this critical hour."[10] But our problem is not
simply that we need to hear the Word proclaimed clearly and correctly, but also that we might actually do something effective on
behalf of others in response. Perhaps a sermon or two on living out
the expository truths taught in James 2 would bridge the gap between this famine of the Word of God that concerns Lawson, and
those who are experiencing a *literal* famine in the land.

> Suppose a brother or sister is without clothes and daily food.
> If one of you says to him, "Go, I wish you well; keep warm
> and well fed," but does nothing about his physical needs,
> what good is it? (James 2:15-16)

Corpses make for poor converts, just as planners—playing with
large sums of money from a safe distance—make for poor plans.
Fighting famine is impossible. But addressing the needs of hungry
people in intelligent ways isn't just possible, it's biblical.

FOR FURTHER REFLECTION

Consider becoming a journalist. "Nobel Prize-winning economist
Amartya Sen has observed that there has never been a famine in a
country with a free press."[11]

Learn about regions of our world undergoing famine. Find specific, local ways to act in partnership with indigenous peoples.
Commit to pray. Identify a small, specific problem, and work with
others to make life better there.

3

Give Drink to the Thirsty

If your enemy is hungry, give him food to eat;
if he is thirsty, give him water to drink.

PROVERBS 25:21

The poor and needy search for water, but there is none;
their tongues are parched with thirst. But I the LORD will
answer them; I, the God of Israel, will not forsake them.
I will make rivers flow on barren heights, and springs
within the valleys. I will turn the desert into pools
of water, and the parched ground into springs.

ISAIAH 41:17-18

IMAGINE YOU THINK this is a chapter worth skipping. The average layperson never thinks about water. And yet in Matthew 25, Jesus specifically commends the "sheep" (those he invites to inherit his kingdom) because "I was thirsty and you gave me something to drink." This is often perceived as simply an example of the kinds of behaviors Christians are to be engaged in—one little way in which we can be of help to others.

People in developed nations hear Jesus say, "If anyone gives even
a cup of cold water to one of these little ones because he is my
disciple, I tell you the truth, he will certainly not lose his reward"
(Matthew 10:42) and immediately think in terms of hospitality. As
one British author puts it, "That 'cup' might mean boiling the kettle
and providing a listening ear."[1] But in point of fact, a cup of safe,
drinkable water is tremendously precious. Water shortages are
common across Africa, to consider just one region: in Somalia,
Rwanda, Kenya, Uganda, Nigeria, Namibia, Zimbabwe, Ethiopia,
Ghana, Sierra Leone, Gambia, South Africa and Mozambique,
people often struggle for water.[2] The World Bank has expressed
concerns regarding the possibility of water wars, but "most organized violence from water conflict occurs not between states, but
at the subnational and local levels or between sectors."[3]

Water is needed for irrigation. Water is needed for basic sani-
tation and hygiene. If we lived when Jesus lived or in an area of
the world where pure water now remains hard to come by, we
would more viscerally understand these verses from Matthew's
Gospel: far more than simple hospitality extended over a cup of
tea, Jesus is calling us to selfless generosity, sometimes with life
and death implications.

Certainly as individuals, we are to show generosity, hospitality
and kindness. But is there nothing more that can be done? In the
previous chapter we considered how concrete, measurable actions
in specific situations were more likely than grand master plans to
produce demonstrable benefits. Paul Polak's book *Out of Poverty*
highlights numerous local actions that can be taken to help the
poor; a substantial proportion of these activities are related to
water.[4] In a wide range of settings, simple methods and tools can
be employed to make irrigation and other water-related solutions
possible; Polak encourages ingenuity in the design of inexpensive
pumps, latrines and other essentials. (Unfortunately, even though

such projects profit humanity—and open doors for the gospel—such projects are not always financially profitable, and so engineers are diverted to other projects.)

So it's left to people motivated by something other than financial profit. Teenager Hannah Salwen considered the plight of one homeless person in her community, and ultimately she led her family to give away half of the proceeds from the sale of their home. They went on to sponsor projects in Ghana (and perhaps elsewhere as well).[5] What motivated the Salwen family? And if they can do it, what can we do? Would giving a cup of cold water in the name of Jesus be too much? When we help meet the physical needs of people who need water, we might also win a hearing to share with them about the Lord Jesus—who spoke of himself as *living* water (cf. John 4).

FOR FURTHER REFLECTION

Take a short-term mission trip to a region with water needs and spend time understanding firsthand what might be of value to the people there. Consider: what's missing? What could be of help? What could be improved?

How could you and your friends at home establish a longer-term partnership with these people? How might your efforts in addressing their water needs open doors for the gospel, which is ultimately our heart's desire?

4

Care for the Stranger

The people of the land practice extortion and commit robbery;
they oppress the poor and needy and mistreat
the alien, denying them justice.

EZEKIEL 22:29

MANY CHRISTIANS HAVE COME TO THINK God is a Republican, while others confidently assert he's a Democrat. It's fair to say, though, that God is the paradigmatic Independent—truly there is none like him, even though he created us in his image and calls us to follow in his footsteps.

Let's apply some independent thinking, then, to the matter of the stranger, the alien, the foreigner living in our midst. Every country needs immigration laws—or so it seems. And in the United States, immigration laws have changed dramatically throughout the country's history. While issues associated with immigration are routinely labeled as complex, there is much that can be learned from Scripture on this topic. But the Bible can really mess with your head if you let it. So some cultural reflection may be helpful at the outset.

Suppose you wake up one fine morning in Tanzania or Sudan or Uruguay or Mexico, and you decide, *Hey! I want to be an American!* Assuming you are a law-abiding soul, free from immediate threats of aggression or starvation or poverty, you may move quickly to this simple question: *How can I apply to live in the United States legally?*

The first thing you'd do is get on the Internet. Never mind that getting on the Internet might pose a challenge to poor or illiterate or otherwise disadvantaged people. But let's assume that you are an industrious sort, and you find the U.S. government's website describing how you can get a green card.[1] Assuming you don't have family in that country or boutique job skills, there is one basic legal path into the United States: the *diversity lottery*.

The diversity lottery distributes a fixed number of green cards, attempting to ensure representation from throughout the world. Out of the 13.6 million people who participated in the 2010 diversity lottery, 102,800 (or .755 percent) were selected and notified. Only some of those "winners" will actually be able to jump through all the subsequent hoops required; ultimately only 50,000 green cards were issued. It's worth mentioning that, depending on a variety of factors (including how many people were allowed to obtain green cards in prior years), many countries are ineligible in certain years to have people apply at all. Which reminds me: if you're from Mexico, you are ineligible to apply at present. Sorry. Try again next year.[2]

On average, then, the typical Tanzanian or Sudanese or Uruguayan with solid Internet access and English-language reading skills who enters the diversity lottery will be a winner every 150 years or so. Let's say life is getting really hard in your home country, and you *lose* the lottery but can somehow get into the United States anyway: wouldn't you be just the slightest bit tempted to try?

There is a stark irony in the way that the United States is increasingly closed to immigrants. Didn't the original European immigrants massacre many of the indigenous North American people? Wouldn't current law stop the Puritans from coming here? How many natural-born American citizens are the children of immigrants? And what do we make of the poem etched on the base of the Statue of Liberty?

Not like the brazen giant of Greek fame,
With conquering limbs astride from land to land
Here at our sea-washed, sunset gates shall stand
A mighty woman with a torch, whose flame
Is the imprisoned lightning, and her name
Mother of Exiles. From her beacon-hand
Glows world-wide welcome; her mild eyes command
The air-bridged harbor that twin cities frame.

"Keep ancient lands, your storied pomp!" cries she
With silent lips. "Give me your tired, your poor,
Your huddled masses yearning to breathe free,
The wretched refuse of your teeming shore.
Send these, the homeless, tempest-tost to me,
I lift my lamp beside the golden door!"

Give me your tired, your poor, your huddled masses yearning to breathe free? The wretched refuse of your teeming shore? Send these, the homeless, tempest-tossed to me? Are we kidding? Don't we mean fewer than 1 percent of them?

That is unless, of course, they're willing to risk their lives to sneak into our country and mow our lawns, pick our lettuce, make our lattes and debone our chickens until they destroy their hands.[3] Amid all the rhetoric about "protecting" national borders, millions of immigrants are already among us. Many of them come from Mexico. As Judith Adler Hellman explains,

> According to the *Pew Hispanic Center Report*, one-third of all foreign-born residents of the United States come from Mexico, and people of Mexican origin—both documented and undocumented—now represent two-thirds of all Hispanics in the United States. In fact, some estimates put the total of undocumented Mexicans at somewhere between 10 and 15 million.[4]

The predicament of the hidden workers living among us is often hopeless: "An analysis of the 2000 census showed that in eighty-five California cities, over 25 percent of the adult population is disenfranchised because they are not citizens. In twelve of these cities, noncitizens are over 50 percent of the adult population."[5] These immigrants, illegal or otherwise, are not only *strangers* and *aliens;* many of them are our neighbors. So for the moment, instead of thinking about the *political* problem of immigration, what about the *spiritual* one?

BLESSING UPON BLESSING

"Welcome to America: We Speak English. Learn it or Leave." This bumper sticker reflects a common American attitude. It is darkly humorous, but it's not biblical. If Jesus ministered to prostitutes and tax collectors (and other sinners), do you think he would have ministered to "illegals"? But according to Aviva Chomsky, the "suggestion that noncitizens, too, are created equal is virtually absent from the public square."[6]

By contrast, Job could say, "I took up the case of the stranger" (Job 29:16), and Solomon taught that "he who is kind to the poor lends to the LORD, and he will reward him for what he has done" (Proverbs 19:17). In the book of Exodus, the people of Israel were warned, "Do not oppress an alien; you yourselves know how it feels to be aliens, because you were aliens in Egypt" (Exodus 23:9).

The people of Israel had spent generations in bondage in Egypt. They knew no life apart from slavery until the spectacular deliverance that God brought about through Moses—the ten plagues and a spectacular superintendence over events which resulted in their ultimate freedom. We who are Christians consider the bondage we have been freed from even greater; we have been freed from a soul-damning bondage to sin. We have received blessing upon blessing, and we have a freedom in Jesus Christ that transcends any earthly status. Indeed, our citizenship is ultimately not in any country on earth but in heaven (cf. Philippians 3:20).

How much more, then, should we have compassion on those who are aliens and strangers from our God? Is this not even a more tragic reality than the temporal situation they might face in their naturalization? Does it not seem obvious that we are called to draw them to Christ far more than we are called to work for their deportation?

None of this discounts the legitimacy of stewarding national resources responsibly and discouraging illegal immigration. But too often conversations about immigration are cast in the abstract; meanwhile, many of our classmates, our coworkers, our neighbors are immigrants. They are real people, not statistics; they are flesh and blood, made in the image of God. They are our neighbors, and whatever we do about immigration is ultimately accountable to Jesus' command to "love your neighbor as yourself" (Mark 12:31).

FOR FURTHER REFLECTION

Teach English as a second language.

Pay the people who work for you a living wage.

Help your local, state and national officials avoid simplistic solutions to immigration issues; introduce Scripture into the public conversation.

Make friends with at least one person for whom English is not his/her mother tongue.

5

Help the Homeless

*He raises the poor from the dust and lifts the needy
from the ash heap; he seats them with princes,
with the princes of their people.*

PSALM 113:7-8

*He who oppresses the poor shows contempt for their Maker,
but whoever is kind to the needy honors God.*

PROVERBS 14:31

EVERY ONE OF THE THIRTY-THREE TOPICS considered in this book has a spiritual dimension. The relationship between homelessness and holiness, in particular is an example of how our call to address social problems may carry spiritual overtones. There are at least three possible trajectories by which to consider homelessness and holiness.

1. Homelessness may be an indication of persistent sin in an individual's life. The apostle Paul directly addresses idleness, for example—something often attributed to homeless people—as a sin:

> In the name of the Lord Jesus Christ, we command you, brothers, to keep away from every brother who is idle and

does not live according to the teaching you received from us. For you yourselves know how you ought to follow our example. We were not idle when we were with you, nor did we eat anyone's food without paying for it. On the contrary, we worked night and day, laboring and toiling so that we would not be a burden to any of you. We did this, not because we do not have the right to such help, but in order to make ourselves a model for you to follow. For even when we were with you, we gave you this rule: "If a man will not work, he shall not eat." We hear that some among you are idle. They are not busy; they are busy-bodies. Such people we command and urge in the Lord Jesus Christ to settle down and earn the bread they eat. (2 Thessalonians 3:6-12)[1]

2. Some people, by contrast, are homeless not because of their sin (or perhaps not exclusively due to their sin) but because of their circumstances. In her book *Without a Net* Michelle Kennedy tells the story of how she and her three children fell quickly from a comfortable life into homelessness.[2] A series of bad decisions contributed to her descent; and yet none of the situations she describes seems any worse than decisions we may have made at one time or another. Stories like hers are neither rare nor unusual, and too often they are ignored and forgotten.

Kennedy's situation is illustrative of how circumstances over which one has little or no control can contribute to the problem of homelessness. A family member's chronic medical condition can result in bankruptcy. A community's economic decline can shutter businesses. An unscrupulous associate can prey on a business partner, leaving mountainous debts. The family one is born into may be impoverished.

Homelessness, by itself, then, is not a spiritual marker any more than blindness. When his disciples asked Jesus, "Who sinned, this man or his parents, that he was born blind?" he responded, "Neither this man nor his parents sinned. . . . But this happened so that the works of God might be displayed in his life" (John 9:2-3).

In such cases, it may be most useful to consider the frequent biblical calls to care for the stranger, the hungry and the poor as our point of connection with holiness: *we,* who are "homeful," are called to be a holy people (1 Peter 2:9), people who strive after holiness (Hebrews 12:14). Perhaps Paul's broad counsel to the Galatians will serve us well in this light: "Therefore, as we have opportunity, let us do good to all people, especially to those who belong to the family of believers" (Galatians 6:10).

3. But there is a third category that must also be considered. Some people are homeless *because* they are holy. One brief snapshot into the life of Jesus, for example, reveals that homelessness was his own reality: "A teacher of the law came to him and said, 'Teacher, I will follow you wherever you go.' Jesus replied, 'Foxes have holes and birds of the air have nests, but the Son of Man has no place to lay his head'" (Matthew 8:19-20). Could Jesus have had a home? Surely. And at various points in the Gospels, we see Jesus enjoying the hospitality of others. But the pattern of his life reflected a conscious choice: foxes and birds had better housing. And while some have been wrong to nearly deify men such as Francis of Assisi, we should not be so quick to dismiss those who have chosen to give their lives in humble service to the poor as he did—they are surely among us.

You will sometimes hear Christians say, "I don't want to give homeless people money because they will just go off and spend it on alcohol or drugs" or "Some people don't deserve help." What we *deserve* is indeed a very important point of consideration. David Brainerd, whose ministry among Native Americans caused him to experience a very real homelessness, observed, "What God designs by all my distresses I know not; but this I know, I deserve them all, and thousands more."[3] Brainerd is acknowledging that, owing to our sin, every human being deserves nothing other than the wrath of God and a destiny in hell. And yet by the great grace and mercy of God, we who have trusted Christ have instead experienced forgiveness. In this light, we who have been forgiven much should be quick to forgive others (cf. Matthew 18:23-35). In any case, it would be wrong to assume that the homeless people we encounter are homeless as a consequence of their sin.

Homelessness is a problem evident in every city in the world. Jennifer Toth describes the situation aptly:

> Homeless people have been called many names and described in many ways—unseen men, forgotten men, derelicts, hobos, vagrants, bums, beggars. They have lived in Hoovervilles, shanty towns, boxcars and sewers. They are a problem in every modern industrialized country today. In Japan, homeless people are called "johatsu," meaning wandering spirit or one who has lost his identity. "They" are not only men, but also women and their children. And they live not only in the streets where you see them but also under the sidewalks where you don't.[4]

Of the various ministry opportunities this book presents, working with the homeless is among the most challenging and even intimidating. While every man, woman and child is made in the image of God, it can be easy to forget this when working with the homeless; there is nothing to mask the smells that are so common, the frequent reality of mental illness, the prevalence of alcohol and drug abuse, and of course the reality of sin. It is often the case that working with the homeless necessitates intimate, personal and at times even frightening interactions. If you are looking for a ministry in which you will routinely be encouraged and thanked, you may want to begin elsewhere. The goal of working with homeless people is not to assuage our own consciences but to provide genuine help to them.[5] The prophet Isaiah encouraged the people of Israel—and us as well—to "provide the poor wanderer with shelter" (Isaiah 58:7).

Since ministry to the homeless is such hard work, and the rewards are few, Jesus' comments to his dinner host may remind us of where our real rewards lie:

> When you give a luncheon or dinner, do not invite your friends, your brothers or relatives, or your rich neighbors; if you do, they may invite you back and so you will be repaid. But when you give a banquet, invite the poor, the crippled, the lame, the blind, and you will be blessed. Although they cannot repay you, you will be repaid at the resurrection of the righteous. (Luke 14:12-14)

FOR FURTHER REFLECTION

A significant proportion of those who are homeless are military veterans. Consider using Veterans Day to mobilize your church community toward greater engagement of the homeless around you.

6

Supply Clothes to the Needy

Rich and poor have this in common:
The LORD is the Maker of them all.

PROVERBS 22:2

I needed clothes and you clothed me.

MATTHEW 25:36

WALK-IN CLOSETS ARE A COMMON FEATURE of suburban US homes. We consider them normal, natural, uninspiring. But walk-in closets are anything but normal. In industrial nations such as Japan, where space is at a premium, hotel rooms the size of a typical walk-in closet would not be unusual. In developing nations, whole families would cheerfully—enthusiastically—live in a space as warm and secure as our walk-in closets.

The great irony is that walk-in closets are often jammed to the rafters with clothes that could dress a dozen villages. We stand in our walk-in closets and complain about needing more room. We find it easy to hold clothing drives in our churches, because there is often so much excess that it generally doesn't hurt to give a few things. Besides, we might be able to wrangle a tax deduction, and we may free up a pinch more space in our bulging closets. (When clothing from these drives makes its way to developing nations, the sizes are often too big for people there to wear.)

One of the ways Jesus distinguished between the sheep and the goats, in Matthew 25, had to do with clothes ("I needed clothes and you clothed me"). It's likely not the case, however, that naked individuals will come up to us and ask specifically for clothing. As such, if we are to provide needed clothes to people, we might have to seek them out.

Consider a few examples:

- Dress for Success (www.dressforsuccess.org) was formed "to promote the economic independence of disadvantaged women by providing professional attire, a network of support and the career development tools to help women thrive in work and in life."

- Toms is a for-profit company that donates a pair of shoes to a child in need every time a pair of shoes is purchased (www.toms.com).[1]

- Global Girlfriend (www.globalgirlfriend.com) has created opportunities for women in poverty to create fair-trade goods. Founder Stacy Edgar writes, "Women do 66 percent of the world's work but earn only 10 percent of the income and own only 1 percent of the property."[2]

- Samaritan's Feet (www.samaritansfeet.org) is a nonprofit organization working with "over four million impoverished children and adults in more than 60 nations being served by having their feet washed, receiving a new pair of shoes, and hearing a message of hope."[3]

If you investigate each of these four enterprises, you will find that only the group known as Samaritan's Feet positions the work they do in a spiritual context. By contrast, churches are generally disinclined to have even thrift shops: they are a lot of work, the clientele is at times difficult to work with, and staffing and storage can be hard to arrange. How much more so for organizations that both preach the gospel and care for physical needs. Helping people in need can require a lot of work, and, like everyone else, Christians are busy people.

It was Jesus, though, who said in commendation, "I needed clothes and you clothed me" and in condemnation, "I needed clothes and you did not clothe me" (Matthew 25:36, 43). We can hear these words and immediately spiritualize them: "I saw the need of that hurting person, and I offered help and care." While there are surely spiritual implications, a very particular concern for the poor is represented in this most pressing need of clothing.

The story of the prodigal son is a particularly vivid illustration of this principle. A son rejects and abandons his father, taking his wealth with him and squandering it. While the father could legitimately act toward that son with justice and rebuke, instead he welcomes the son home in spectacular fashion:

> Quick! Bring the best robe and put it on him. Put a ring on his finger and sandals on his feet. Bring the fattened calf and kill it. Let's have a feast and celebrate. For this son of mine was dead and is alive again; he was lost and is found. (Luke 15:22-24)

Redemption and regalia intertwine. God is not content to *merely* clothe his children; he bedecks them in the righteousness of Christ himself.

If the father in this story represents God, clothing the naked, who does the older brother represent? He has his wealth and is in fact driven by it, so much so that he refuses to show compassion to his brother. The response of the father to this wealthy son is remarkable; the son comes across to the reader as someone to be pitied. In his book *The Rich, the Poor and the Bible*, Conrad Boerma asserts that in fact God himself is pleading the cause of the poor; it is we who are rich who may be in need.

> Power, money, possessions, other people, authority and love are necessary because there are those who feel that they are nothing without them. That is why the Bible is never sorry for the poor. It takes their side and *pleads their cause*. It is sorry for the rich. What a pity you are rich! Luke's "woes" in chapter 6 of his gospel do not have moralistic implications. They are an *expression of Jesus' pity*. We say, "What a pity about the poor!" Jesus says precisely the opposite. "Blessed are the poor. What a pity about the rich!"[4]

This is a book about imagination and action. As has been seen in this chapter, there are many with lesser motivations than that of the Christian church who are engaged in the creative transformation of the lives of the poor. Will we seek to meet with God for the purpose of living out his commands relating to serving the poor? It is God himself pleading their cause. Will we listen?

FOR FURTHER REFLECTION

Service projects are increasingly common in school settings. Some groups provide prom dresses to those who otherwise would not have one.[5] Is this akin to clothing the naked? Perhaps not. But it is illustrative of kindness offered to others that meets the spirit of the law, if not the letter.

7

Care for the Sick

I was sick and you looked after me.

MATTHEW 25:36

A CHILD HAS STREP THROAT. Your spouse needs a colonoscopy. Your mother must get blood work done. Your father's blood pressure is up again. Driving back and forth to doctors' appointments, going to the drugstore, back to the doctor for follow-ups. These are wearing duties. Unglamorous duties. Duties that bring little prestige. Our culture doesn't value this use of time all that much. Try going into detail about somebody's medical condition, and you will see eyes glaze over. And yet, these situations are all-consuming when you are in the midst of them. Somebody has to tend to them.

The impulse to look after others runs deep. And though caregiving is tiring, it surely also brings a sense of purpose and meaning. Thomas Moore rightly observes that "care of home and family gives back vast amounts of feeling and imagination to the soul."[1]

In the judgment of contemporary American culture, however, the kind of self-abnegation involved with caregiving is weakness. American culture says: "Just do it." "Follow your dreams." "Take care of yourself." Never do we hear this advice: "Put yourself last."

What if self-abnegation is not a weakness but a strength? Anyone who has experience with caregiving knows that it is a test of stamina, resolve and patience. It takes all that we have to develop a daily routine. Personal care tasks. Home management tasks. Doctors' visits. All of this is extremely time-consuming, not to mention stressful. Our world becomes defined by illness management. There is very little "me time."

The Bible is filled with stories about sick people. Lepers. Paralytics. Demoniacs. People who were lame or blind. Read the Gospels, and it's clear that Jesus spends a lot of time with the sick. They press against him, make demands on him, even drop down through holes in the ceiling before him. How does Jesus respond? As Jesus interacts with the sick, he demonstrates for us the spiritual dimensions of caregiving.

Illness is no respecter of persons. The biblical accounts of sick people prove this point, as illness falls like a hard rain on people of all stations.

- On the daughter of a ruler of the synagogue, Jairus (Mark 5:21-43)

- On the servant of a centurion (Matthew 8:5-13)

- On a poor widow's son (Luke 7:11-17)

Jesus is surrounded by people with needs, some of them seemingly hopeless cases. Chronic cases, like the woman who had an issue of blood for twelve years (Mark 5:25-34) or the woman who had been crippled for eighteen years (Luke 13:10-17). In each case, Jesus faces a person who has brought a broken body and often a broken spirit before him. Sick people are usually discouraged people. They've sought help and gotten nowhere. They come across as needy. They can be unpleasant. Querulous.

Jesus does not shrink from such people. Indeed, Jesus uses his ministry to the sick to reveal important dimensions of who he is.

Sick people begin to feel faceless and ignored. Doctors notoriously talk at the sick, not to them. In the midst of difficult discussions, doctors often choose to talk with the family rather than the ill person. In contrast, Jesus engages the sick, speaking with them, touching them.

Let's take a look at one case: the woman who had struggled with her illness for twelve years.

> And a woman was there who had been subject to bleeding for twelve years. She had suffered a great deal under the care of many doctors and had spent all she had, yet instead of getting better she grew worse. When she heard about Jesus, she came up behind him in the crowd and touched his cloak, because she thought, "If I just touch his clothes, I will be healed." Immediately her bleeding stopped and she felt in her body that she was freed from her suffering.
>
> At once Jesus realized that power had gone out from him. He turned around in the crowd and asked, "Who touched my clothes?"
>
> "You see the people crowding against you," his disciples answered, "and yet you can ask, 'Who touched me?'"
>
> But Jesus kept looking around to see who had done it. Then the woman, knowing what had happened to her, came and fell at his feet and, trembling with fear, told him the whole truth. He said to her, "Daughter, your faith has healed you. Go in peace and be freed from your suffering." (Mark 5:25-34)

The first thing to notice here is that the woman is not even named. She's generic; she could be any sick person who has tried it all. The Bible says that she has suffered under the care of doctors and had used up her resources, and yet she has gotten not better but worse. This woman might have resigned herself, but she decides to try one more thing. And this time Jesus makes it count. Pressed by the crowd, Jesus nevertheless stops and addresses this woman who in desperation has come to him for healing. And Jesus, being God, heals her.

Jesus shows us what to do. Modeling attention and concern, he does not protect himself from the ill. He surrounds himself with people who need things from him. He makes himself available. He goes among them; he touches them. He asks them what they need.

Early in the Gospel of Mark we read an account of the life of Jesus that sounds particularly down-to-earth, one that seems common to every home. Peter's mother-in-law is sick, in bed with a fever. It could have been the common cold. The sniffles. The flu. Who knows?

The disciples set a good example for us by going to Jesus on behalf of this woman, even though the situation does not appear as grave as many of the other physical maladies that Jesus dealt with. And Jesus sets an example for us here as well. The Scripture says, "He went to her, took her hand and helped her up. The fever left her and she began to wait on them" (Mark 1:31).

You and I do not possess in ourselves the capacity to heal that Jesus did (although charlatans abound). That said, Jesus' example here is noteworthy in several respects. He listens to the concern, cares enough to intervene, takes the woman's hand. There is great significance to this gesture. Startlingly, to people like us for whom hand-washing is all the rage (and probably should be), Jesus displays an utter lack of self-regard.

A physical touch for the sick is often of immeasurable benefit. A woman with HIV/AIDS once said, "Sometimes I have a terrible feeling that I am dying not from the virus, but from being untouchable."[2] Rachel Remen, a doctor who works with adults who have cancer, says they "often feel as though they are merely a 'piece of meat.'" She reports that one woman said, "Sometimes when I go for my chemotherapy, they touch me as if they don't know anybody's inside the body."[3]

Remen goes on to refer to a study "to explore the effects of touch on infants so small they could be held in one hand. Half the infants were touched (gently rubbing the baby's back with a pinkie finger) for fifteen minutes every few hours. Those babies were more likely to survive than the ones who were not touched."[4] As such the minor mention in Mark's Gospel about Jesus touching Peter's mother-in-law is freighted with import. And of course, Jesus heals her, the hope we would have for all who struggle with health issues.

It's probably a reach to say that there is also significance to the record in Mark's Gospel that as Jesus was healing Peter's mother-in-law, he also "helped her up." Still, the image is certainly evocative of the kind of subtle, humble, often unseen care that one human can give another. In our daily lives, we will not lack opportunities to minister to the sick. It is guaranteed that we will have opportunities to serve family members, friends, coworkers, and neighbors. For some of us, this is relatively easy and natural. For others, it will require an effort. We will not always achieve sainthood. But if we allow ourselves to see driving an elderly neighbor to the doctor as a spiritual act, it will be a spiritual act.

In accepting inconvenience and in embracing such service, we will be following the example of Jesus. Along the way, we will be blessed.

FOR FURTHER REFLECTION

Volunteer at a local hospital.

Monitor the prayer list in your church bulletin and write cards and visit the sick.

Encourage your children to pray for friends and family who are ill.

Become involved with a ministry to children with HIV/AIDS.[5]

8

Provide Disaster Relief

*You have been a refuge for the poor, a refuge for
the needy in their distress, a shelter from
the storm and a shade from the heat.*

ISAIAH 25:4

MANY AMERICANS PROBABLY HAVE more personal experience of tornados than any other kind of storm. We know the drill: get in a hallway or a bathroom and crouch until it's over. If the winds are too strong, we might have to deal with uprooted trees or with roof damage. Luckily, Nationwide is on our side; we will file a property damage report, and the tree people or the roof people will come and get things back to normal. Recently, a couple at a school concert were talking as if water in the basement of their beach house—their second house, mind you—was a problem.

If we are being honest with ourselves, many of us really can't relate to those who have endured truly devastating tornadoes, earthquakes, hurricanes and other truly calamitous events. In August 2005 the world was transfixed as Hurricane Katrina hit the Gulf Coast, creating what Rev. Nelson Johnson has called a "tragedy of biblical and constitutional proportions."[1] Rachel Luft explains what a middle-class response might be:

So you've never evacuated from a natural disaster before, and don't know what it's like. . . . You've never gone to sleep your first night in a new apartment without a bed, a couch, towels, or a can opener. You've never had a neighbor email you to tell you a tree had crashed through your roof, never lost every handpicked picture frame, the ceramic lamp your mother gave you on your sweet sixteenth birthday, the letter from your friend Pat who died the year before, the brand new bottle of face cream you never even opened, the bulging folder of medical records. . . . You can't get your mind for one second around the experience of being unable to find your family members. . . . But you did see the pictures on television, and they were as confusing as they were painful. People staggering around in shock, mostly dark people, clutching children, showing the signs of relentless heat exposure, their surroundings surreal and violent: rooftops torn off, evil water up to the throat, immense Southern oaks tangled with power lines lying across roads and buildings, fires burning on water, men in and out of uniform walking with guns. This can't be America.[2]

The real challenge with disasters is that they remind us how very small we are. Americans have tended from the beginning to be a self-reliant lot. We're a nation of individualists who like to march to the beat of our own drum. When we are rocked like the folks in New Orleans were rocked, we realize that our survival depends on community. We're not good at that.

In a global context, we are an anomaly. People who live in the Majority World have a different sense of normal. People know that it's necessary to reach out to others, to stand and fall with them.

Natural disasters are multi-pronged, leaving layers of consequences in their wake. First, there are the physical, material effects. Floods leave standing water and sludge; earthquakes leave rubble;

hurricanes leave buildings demolished. People who find themselves victims to such events are suddenly homeless, or living in homes that are unlivable. Water damage is particularly challenging; contaminated water means bacteria; standing water in homes means mold. Walls and flooring may be compromised. Sometimes the house must be gutted before repairs can even begin. Sifting and sorting must be done. What can be salvaged? What must be thrown out? People who have lost their homes are vulnerable in every way. In Maslow's hierarchy of needs, shelter is near the very top. Victims feel rightly as if their very foundation has been shaken, their patterns of life destroyed in an instant. Add to that the physical toll of disaster waiting in line with the many others who need the same things they do: access to relief agencies, immediate housing, food, water.

Organizations like the Red Cross (www.redcross.org) or Baptist Men on Mission (www.bmen.net) can be a lifeline when disaster strikes. Volunteers get on buses or in vans and go to the site of the disaster, bringing tools, supplies, water, food. Stations are set up. Crews are dispatched. No matter how minimal the skill level of the workers, there's a job for everyone pouring hot coffee, dispensing ice, assisting with baby needs and the like. Folks skilled in construction have all the work they can do. Roofs, walls, floors—all need attention. Church members who have been a part of such efforts report tremendous satisfaction in being able to make a real difference in people's lives.

Along with the material challenges, there are emotional challenges. Families going through the worst of a disaster see everything they've worked for in ruin. Their ravaged homes are a symbol of their now-ravaged lives. There's no wonder that counselors are called in. Children are scared. So are their parents. When the ordinary elements of life are no longer in place—we don't know where we will sleep or when we will eat—stress becomes endemic. The mental energy that we can usually call up for work is now deployed just to survive. Psychological distress becomes the new normal.

People who have hit rock bottom have spiritual needs as well. Volunteers report meaningful interactions with families who have seen their homes destroyed. These families see folks show up at their door, ready and able to help them, and they want to know why. They often cannot fathom that complete strangers have taken time away from their jobs and their families, driving hundreds of miles from their homes, just to lend a hand. This kind of situation provides a unique opportunity for spiritual growth.

Interview anyone who regularly helps with these kinds of efforts. While Christians often lament that people are not open to discussions about faith, those who help bring comfort when disaster strikes will attest to the spiritual openness people evince when they've lost everything.

Does the Bible address disaster? In some ways, the story of Job is a story of disaster. Job loses his crops, his livestock, his servants, his children, his health. When Job cries out in pain and confusion, the voice of God teaches Job through a whirlwind.

> Do you know the laws of the heavens?
> Can you set up God's dominion over the earth?
>
> Can you raise your voice to the clouds
> and cover yourself with a flood of water?
> Do you send the lightning bolts on their way?
> Do they report to you, "Here we are"?
> Who has endowed the heart with wisdom
> or gave understanding to the mind?
> Who has the wisdom to count the clouds?
> Who can tip over the water jars of the heavens
> when the dust becomes hard
> and the clods of earth stick together?

Do you hunt the prey for the lioness
and satisfy the hunger of the lions
when they crouch in their dens
or lie in wait in a thicket?
Who provides food for the raven
when its young cry out to God
and wander about for lack of food? (Job 38:33-41)

God reminds Job of his human condition. Job cannot know the mysteries of the universe. He cannot control nature. His only recourse is to recognize his estate and to turn, with confidence, to God, the author of all creation.

At the end of the book, Job is restored, materially and spiritually. People who are at their most vulnerable are often the most open to spiritual growth. Volunteers who take the time to engage in deep conversation with hurting people have a real opportunity to lead them in a new and positive direction. Rebuilding their homes, they can also lead in the rebuilding of their spirits.

FOR FURTHER REFLECTION

Sign up for a trip to an area affected by disaster. No special training needed.

9

Minister to the Imprisoned

*The LORD hears the needy and does not
despise his captive people.*

PSALM 69:33

*Do not gloat when your enemy falls;
when he stumbles, do not let your heart rejoice,
or the LORD will see and disapprove and
turn his wrath away from him.*

PROVERBS 24:18

*The righteous care about justice for the poor,
but the wicked have no such concern.*

PROVERBS 29:7

*If a king judges the poor with fairness,
his throne will always be secure.*

PROVERBS 29:14

F OR A MOMENT, IMAGINE YOU have been convicted of a crime.
Many people—if not most people—have committed crimes they were not caught for:

- The college freshman who got away with carrying and smoking marijuana is little different from the college freshman who got caught carrying and smoking marijuana.

- The young woman who had one drink too many and somehow drove home safely is little different from the young woman who had one drink over the legal limit and was arrested for driving under the influence.

- The difference between a sexual relationship with someone who is eighteen years old and someone who only looks eighteen years old can mean the difference between an unspiritual sexual encounter and an unspiritual sexual encounter that leads to jail time and sexual offender status.

- You share most of the truth on your taxes one year and are never caught in your half-truths. Contrast this with the man or woman who is found out.

- If you own a gun, what exactly are the laws governing gun possession in your community? Ignorance of this point—often a highly complicated one in some localities—could easily lead to a crime of one kind or another.

- One missed child support payment can put you in jail.

Someone I know recently got a ticket for running a red light. (Her family doesn't know about this episode, and so the matter will still be our little secret.) She was not pulled over by a police officer; a camera took her picture as she ran the light. With advances in technology, countless infractions that went undetected years ago will increasingly result in prosecution. Not all of those infractions result in jail time, but some of them do.

Regardless of your story, one bad decision in your life could result in thoroughgoing punishment. People go to jail every day—even some for crimes they did not commit. It's easy to be skeptical when we hear their story told, but imagine that you find yourself with a criminal record. What kind of a world do you now live in?

1. Whenever you fill out a job application, you have to answer "yes" to the question about whether or not you have committed a crime. Do you think this will help your chances of employment? Roughly 80 percent of employers conduct background checks, and your employment will be terminated if you are found to have lied on your application. It will always be easier for an employer to hire a person without a criminal record than to take a chance on you. In fact, some companies have blanket policies that prevent the hiring of convicted felons.

2. Voting rights, the right to hold public office, the right to bear arms, the right to travel to many countries—these and countless other issues will always come into stark relief if you have been convicted of a crime.

3. Even your ability to volunteer in many settings—including churches—will be greatly impeded by a criminal record, since most volunteer organizations conduct a background check.

Here is the terrifying, horrifying reality: no nation on the face of the earth imprisons a higher proportion of its population than the United States—by a wide margin.

Between 1980 and 1998, the prison population ballooned from 329,821 to 1,302,019—a rise of 295 percent. The increase was so great that by 1998, the number of citizens incarcerated in state and federal prisons exceeded or approximated the resident populations of thirteen states and was larger than all of our major cities with the exceptions of

Chicago, Houston, Los Angeles, New York and Philadelphia. The incarceration rate (number of persons in state and federal prison on any given day per 100,000 population) increased during the same time period from 138 to 461, as compared to only 26 in 1850.[1]

Things have dramatically worsened in the years since that paragraph was written: our incarceration rate has exploded to 716 per 100,000 population, and 2,239,751 are now in prison—one out of every 139 people in the country. Figure 9.1 helps illustrate the point vividly.

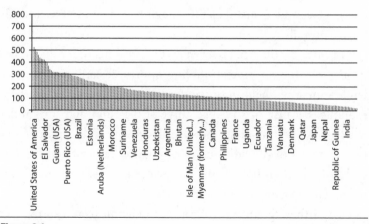

Figure 9.1.

The United States imprisons a far higher proportion of its own population than Rwanda, Cuba, Iran, Pakistan, China or the Russian Republic. While other nations have been more violent toward its own people, and short-term issues have arisen at different points in human history, it is not a dramatic leap to make the case that the United States at present is among the most intrusive police states in the history of humankind. By contrast, Canada imprisons roughly seven times less of its population. Is it because Canadians are dramatically less prone to crime? Is Canada seven times nicer? American political rhetoric often includes lamentations over human rights violations in other parts of the world, but we may be culpable for more such violations than any other nation.

The prison industry in the United States is quite naturally motivated to imprison as many people as possible, and they have a powerful lobbying presence in Washington, D.C. The United States has built many more prisons and has many more laws that send people to prison for longer periods of time than other parts of the world. Compounding matters, it is quite difficult to get elected if one is perceived as insufficiently tough on crime. And as a result, lunacy prevails.

Consider the financial burden overimprisonment results in, not to mention the far more troubling human costs. Nonviolent offenders are often held in prison for extensive periods of time, for example, because of so-called three strike rules and for similar reasons. While it's surely the case that we need to improve our prison model to provide true rehabilitation rather than to focus primarily on punishment, the far greater issue is evident: we imprison far too many people to begin with.

One further agonizing realization to take in relates to the fact that the statistics vary widely based on ethnicity:

The imprisonment rates indicate that about 0.5% of all white males, more than 3.0% of all black males, and 1.2% of all Hispanic males were imprisoned in 2011. Between 6.6% and 7.5% of all black males ages 25 to 39 were imprisoned in 2011, which were the highest imprisonment rates among the measured sex, race, Hispanic origin, and age groups. Slightly fewer than 3% of Hispanic males were imprisoned in each of the age cohorts between ages 25 and 39.[2]

In some cities, an astonishing 80 percent of the adult black male workforce has a felony record.[3] We wring our hands when we hear such statistics, wondering what, if anything, can be done.

Most Christians think of prison ministry as church services held in prisons. As good as these may be, clearly, much more must be done. James Orbinski observes, "A few weeks after I returned from Zaire in January 1997, I went to see Benedict [a counselor friend]. 'Justice is an illusion,' I said as we walked through the woods. 'Not when you know what injustice is,' Benedict replied immediately. 'The victim is someone quite concrete. Justice only fails when we fail to imagine that it is possible. But like so many things, it depends not only on imaginings but on what we do.'"[4] Put bluntly, "The cages must be dismantled."[5]

FOR FURTHER REFLECTION

If you are in a position to hire, then hire a qualified candidate with a criminal record. The loyalty this individual will have will exceed anyone else on your staff.

If you are not in a position to hire, become involved with an organization that helps those who are released from prison get jobs. Make it a goal to help just one person in this way.

10

Effectively Oppose Abortion

If you say, "But we knew nothing about this," does not he who weighs the heart perceive it? Does not he who guards your life know it? Will he not repay each person according to what he has done?

PROVERBS 24:12

"Because of the oppression of the weak and the groaning of the needy, I will now arise," says the LORD. "I will protect them from those who malign them."

PSALM 12:5

IT MAY SEEM OUT OF PLACE IN A BOOK on mercy ministries to include a brief chapter on the subject of abortion, but my rationale is simple: if we are passionate about showing mercy to the hungry, to the imprisoned, to the sick, to the struggling, our passion must extend also to those whose lives are being poured out by the millions around the world. Abortion is government-sanctioned violence against its most helpless citizens. Christians must remain resolute in opposing all such violence.

We tend to look back in history and label as barbaric ancient practices such as exposing infants to the elements—leaving them in the cold to die. Currently, China's policy to restrict families to only one child is rightly considered horrific.[1] Years from now, will the world recognize the equally horrific, barbaric nature of abortion? As Mother Teresa put it in 1994,

> What is taking place in America is a war against the child. And if we accept that the mother can kill her own child, how can we tell other people not to kill one another? . . . Any country that accepts abortion is not teaching its people to love, but to use any violence to get what they want.[2]

Many Christians lack energy in the battle against abortion because we think it is not a "winnable" issue. "Winnability" is not our criterion, however. Winnability wasn't William Wilberforce's criteria when he fought against slavery in England, and it must not be our criteria now.

But what can be done? Instead of emphasizing only an opposition to abortion, my two favorite actions are positive: crisis pregnancy support and adoption. Those outside the church who accuse the church of not putting its money where its mouth is are right if we cannot act energetically in these two areas. (Each is given its own chapter in this book.)

That said, some other forms of nonviolent protest remain appropriate. I have participated in silent protests where Christians stand holding hands in long chains, displaying signs that remind those who pass by about the sanctity of life. Others may choose to lobby policymakers who, in other situations, may proclaim their deep affection for children.

On December 14, 2012, a gunman opened fire at Sandy Hook Elementary School in Newtown, Connecticut, killing twenty children and six adults. All of the children were between the ages of six and seven. The national outcry over this atrocity was palpable, deep and real. President Obama offered the following perspective:

> The majority of those who died today were children—beautiful little kids between the ages of 5 and 10 years old. They had their entire lives ahead of them—birthdays, graduations, weddings, kids of their own. Among the fallen were also teachers—men and women who devoted their lives to helping our children fulfill their dreams.
>
> So our hearts are broken today—for the parents and grandparents, sisters and brothers of these little children, and for the families of the adults who were lost. Our hearts are broken for the parents of the survivors as well, for as blessed as they are to have their children home tonight, they know that their children's innocence has been torn away from them too early, and there are no words that will ease their pain.[3]

Our hearts must, as the president rightly asserts, be broken. Such senseless violence. He is correct to direct our mind's eye toward all of the missed opportunities for love and service—"birthdays, graduations, weddings, kids of their own." In such unthinkable moments we must weep, grieve, pray and console.

It seems to me, however, that as a nation we cannot truly grieve about Newtown while, at the same time, turning a blind eye toward the daily deaths of thousands. We must let the horror of Newtown and other senseless shootings remind us to "speak up for those who cannot speak for themselves, for the rights of all who are destitute. Speak up and judge fairly; defend the rights of the poor and needy" (Proverbs 31:9).

FOR FURTHER REFLECTION

Seek to save "just" one life—and go from there.

11

Offer Crisis Pregnancy Support

Do not withhold good from those who deserve it, when it is
in your power to act. Do not say to your neighbor,
"Come back later; I'll give it tomorrow"—
when you have it now with you.

PROVERBS 3:27-28

I F YOU TALK TO MOST PARENTS, they will say—gushing—that the day
their child was born was among the very best days of their lives.
They can remember every detail of the labor, of the trip to the
hospital and of the delivery. Detailed measurements of the baby are
noted. Apgar scores are recorded. Scores of pictures are shared.
Celebratory cigars are smoked. Phone calls, texts and posts of
every kind flood out. Many of these same parents shared the news
of their pregnancy in sometimes dramatic ways. Tears of joy were
shed. In a Christian context, prayers of praise and thanksgiving
would quite naturally have been offered. It is hard to imagine how
life could be much better than this.

Contrast this with the reaction an unmarried teenage girl
might experience if she becomes pregnant. The weight of anguish
is impossible to fathom. Perhaps she knows that when a young
woman finds out she is pregnant outside of wedlock (or even

outside of a committed relationship), empathy, patience and understanding are all too often in short supply. Judgment and scorn are all too common. Indeed, she may be subject to abuse from a father or boyfriend.

If all of us always reaped the full measure of what we deserved, what would our lives look like? A friend of mine tells the following story:

> I got pregnant as a freshman in high school. I had sex just once for the first time and used protection. I found out I was pregnant a few months later. I was kicked off the basketball team, even though I had a doctor's note which would have allowed me to still play. My dreams faded slowly, but some of these things were not what God intended for my life. He had other plans, and brought a precious gift into my life, my daughter.
>
> I was brought up in a Christian home, and we went to church every Sunday and Wednesday. When everyone in church found out, I was the gossip on everyone's lips. I was called horrible names; it was as if I had become a virus. Most of my friends left me, because their parents thought I was a bad influence. All I had left was my family and that part of the church family that stood by me.
>
> I became very depressed and had to go to a doctor for help. If people had not treated me that way I would not have put myself down so much. I did stay in school while being a single mother, living with my grandparents who provided for me. I graduated in the top ten of my class as a National Honor Society student. I proved to everyone in that small town that I could still be better than the other teen mothers that dropped out or were not there for their kids. As Christians we should look past the mistakes people make. We need to learn from

them. God forgave me and that's all that counts. We should not judge teen mothers or fathers, instead, we should come alongside of them as Jesus Christ would.

So far as sexuality is concerned, there are many who sit comfortably on cushioned seats in their churches who may not have become pregnant or impregnated another not because they were models of sanctity but because their birth control was effective. Too many of us are quick to point to the sins of others, little realizing how we ourselves have been the recipients of mercy upon mercy—if not in this domain, in countless others (cf. Matthew 18:21-35).

While the church loudly trumpets its opposition to the sin of abortion, ironically unmarried women who find themselves pregnant in such churches may be increasingly tempted toward abortion. It takes great courage for a young unmarried woman to carry a child to term, especially when it may be that all through the pregnancy, she will have to agonize about whether or not to give the child up for adoption or to raise the baby on her own. Her own family may remove her financial support. Her boyfriend or parents may press her hard to have an abortion. One would hope that there would be no more supportive institution on the face of the earth when a woman is in a crisis pregnancy than the church, but as we have seen, this is not always the case.

It's not just young, unmarried teenage women who experience what we would call a crisis pregnancy. Imagine you are a married woman, forty years of age, working two jobs to help your family get by, struggling mightily to make ends meet. What would you do if you became pregnant unexpectedly? Would your first thought be celebration? A woman in a situation such as this might well be afraid of how her husband or loved ones would react. Feel for a moment how difficult it would be to overcome the financial and personal impact that a pregnancy may have in this already fragile home. Who can she turn to for help?

If the first great challenge rests on the woman undergoing a crisis pregnancy, the second great challenge relates to those who might, in fact, want to help. Crisis pregnancy support is not a glamorous ministry; instead, it is among the most personally costly ministries one can engage in. It requires substantial capital and, quite often, the commitment of many volunteers. Consider a partial list of the things a full-orbed crisis pregnancy center might need:

- Trained counselors, perhaps available twenty-four hours a day via phone or chat
- Office space and administration
- Pregnancy testing and medically trained staff for sonograms, screening for STDs and similar prenatal services
- Cribs, car seats, baby clothes, diapers, baby food and myriad other baby supplies
- Maternity clothes
- Furniture
- Adoption counseling and information
- Birthmother housing
- Legal support
- Potential financial assistance to birthmothers
- Child-rearing resources
- Support groups
- Counseling for others connected with the pregnancy
- An Internet presence, potentially including the use of social media
- Post-abortion counseling

A ministry that features even a small proportion of these services is daunting to begin and even more difficult to maintain. It's easy to raise money for missions; it's hard to raise money for the items on this list.

One needs extraordinary motivation to become involved in pregnancy support. One of the most frequently cited passages in Scripture affirming the sanctity of life provides such motivation:

> For you created my inmost being; you knit me together in my mother's womb. I praise you because I am fearfully and wonderfully made; your works are wonderful, I know that full well. My frame was not hidden from you when I was made in the secret place. When I was woven together in the depths of the earth, your eyes saw my unformed body. All the days ordained for me were written in your book before one of them came to be. (Psalm 139:13-16)

Each human being, born and unborn, is precious to Almighty God. We see God's tender care as we are each knit together in our mother's womb. What a contrast this presents to a church that, at times, can be hardened against those who are undergoing unplanned pregnancies. The message of Jesus echoes here: "Whatever you did for the least of these . . . you did for me" (Matthew 25:40).

But saving babies, as wonderful an outcome as that may be, is not the only goal. Think of the greatest challenges you have faced in your own life. In some cases, someone else was there for you in a profound way. It may be that you didn't even know your benefactor. How much did their many kindnesses mean to you? Do you still remember their service as a gift to you from God himself? What about other instances where perhaps no one was there when you needed help? How did you feel?

It is a lot of work to help women in crisis pregnancies. But there are few situations in life more pressing, where help is more needed.

FOR FURTHER REFLECTION

Open a browser on your computer and type the words "Crisis Pregnancy" and the name of the town or city you live in. If one exists in your community, prayerfully consider how you might be involved.

If there is no such service in your community, brainstorm with some friends how you might help get one started.

12

Adopt

> *Whoever heard me spoke well of me,*
> *and those who saw me commended me,*
> *because I rescued the poor who cried for help,*
> *and the fatherless who had none to assist him.*

JOB 29:11-12

> *He will defend the afflicted among the people*
> *and save the children of the needy;*
> *he will crush the oppressor.*

PSALM 72:4

> *Defend the cause of the weak and fatherless;*
> *maintain the rights of the poor and oppressed.*

PSALM 82:3

A COUPLE OF YEARS AGO, I was presented with an unexpected per-spective on adoption. A woman told me that she believed all adoption is wrong.

She didn't go into the details behind her rationale on the subject, but it's always good to hear dissenting views, since they compel you to think. I found her perspective even more provocative because she herself had been adopted. So, reflection is warranted: is adoption really a good thing?

A THEOLOGICAL PERSPECTIVE

There are only a handful of points in Scripture where the topic of adoption is explicitly mentioned:

> The word *adoption* (the Greek means "instating as a son") appears only five times [in the New Testament], and of these occurrences only three refer to the Christian's present relationship to God in Christ (Rom 8:15; Gal 4:5; Eph 1:5). Yet the thought itself is the nucleus and focal point of the whole New Testament teaching on the Christian life.[1]

Paul's letter to the church at Ephesus includes the most pointed mention of adoption: "For he chose us in him before the creation of the world to be holy and blameless in his sight. In love he predestined us *to be adopted as his sons* through Jesus Christ, in accordance with his pleasure and will—to the praise of his glorious grace, which he has freely given us in the One he loves" (Ephesians 1:4-6). From this one passage, a critical observation is possible: if God himself is an adoptive parent, it seems reasonable to assume that Christian adoption would honor him.

There is, in fact, no point in Scripture where the concept of adoption is cast in a negative light. When Mordecai is mentioned in Scripture, for example, the text simply explains that he had adopted Esther. This does not appear to be unusual, but an expression of caring concern (cf. Esther 2:15).

The doctrine of adoption is often featured as an important one in the so-called *ordo salutis*, a theological construct that reflects on the various aspects of a Christian's progress ranging from the new birth to glorification. In this construct, adoption uniquely touches on the inheritance and intimacy that believers enjoy as they are brought into the family of God. Ironically, though, this doctrine is almost universally ignored by Christian writers. J. I. Packer explains,

> It is a strange fact that the truth of adoption has been little regarded in Christian history. Apart from two nineteenth-century books, now scarcely known (R. S. Candlish, *The Fatherhood of God*; R. A. Webb, *The Reformed Doctrine of Adoption*), there is no evangelical writing on it, nor has there been at any time since the Reformation, any more than there was before. Luther's grasp of adoption was as strong and clear as his grasp of justification, but his disciples held to the latter and made nothing of the former. The Puritan teaching on the Christian life, so strong in other ways, was notably deficient here, which is one reason why legalistic misunderstandings of it so easily arise. Perhaps the early Methodists, and later Methodist saints like Billy Bray, "the King's Son," with his unforgettable approach to prayer—"I must talk to Father about this"—came closest to the life of sonship as the New Testament depicts it. There is certainly more to make of adoption in Christian teaching today.[2]

For Packer, adoption is no ancillary matter: "You sum up the whole of New Testament teaching in a single phrase, if you speak of it as a revelation of the Fatherhood of the holy Creator. In the same way, you sum up the whole of New Testament religion if you describe it as the knowledge of God as one's holy Father."[3] He adds that adoption "is the *highest privilege that the gospel offers:* higher even than justification."[4]

While it is true that the emphasis in the New Testament is on a spiritual form of adoption, rather than on that of parents adopting children, Christian adoption is consistent with the character of God (as has been seen) and is also consistent with the notion that care be extended to "the least of these" (Matthew 25:40). While it is prudent to acknowledge that adoption has at times been pursued with questionable motives,[5] this is true of all human endeavors. While great care must be exercised, adoption must be presented in the church as a God-honoring venture that should be encouraged.

THREE VANTAGE POINTS

Many Americans do not think carefully about what it means to grow up in the foster care system, much less to consider what it means to be an orphan in another country. Reflect on this for a moment: what would it mean if you had not grown up with a connection to a mother, father or other permanent caregiver? In what ways would your life be different? Now, consider the other side of the coin: if you were to adopt a child, how would that child's life be altered?

Harold Myra offers the very personal perspective of a father considering an international adoption:

> In the Dominican Republic we visited a school with hundreds of lively children who eagerly gathered around us. Somehow, exploring, I got separated from the others. I was gazing out at the ocean when a woman, perhaps a teacher, quietly called to me. She was saying something to me about a baby. I was caught off guard and didn't understand. She kept talking until finally I realized she was offering me a child.[6]

This experience is far less rare than might be imagined. Children themselves will often, as they grow older, passionately urge foreigners to adopt them.

Myra was able to recognize the scope of the problem: "I knew that not far from this cavernous court building was a hospital with scores of unwanted black babies. Babies ready to bond and love, stuck in hospital cribs, destined for the system because they weren't the right color."[7] After prayer and reflection, the Myra family made their decision: "Life is full of risks, and in faith we make our judgments as best we can. I called Jeanette and told her I thought we should go ahead with the adoption."[8]

Tom Davis advocates passionately for adoption in his book *Fields of the Fatherless: Discover the Joy of Compassionate Living.*

> In recent years, ministering in the fields of the fatherless hasn't been as much of a priority to the church as it has been throughout history. Many well-intentioned believers have lost sight of what God cares about most. The fact is, we put most of our energy into what is improving the four walls of our churches rather than bringing in the harvest that is outside.[9]

Ultimately, it is God himself who quickens the hearts of believers to respond to this calling:

> While every adoption experience is unique, one word seems to speak to the ways in which children and families are brought together: *convergence*. I believe once people open or lend themselves to the idea of adoption, God works in miraculous ways to bring about the desire of His heart: the grand orchestration of setting the loneliest of His Children in a loving, caring family.[10]

Perhaps most moving is the real-life struggle of the Ethiopian woman Haregewoin Teferra, whose story has been brought to light through the efforts of Melissa Fay Greene.[11] Teferra was living a typical enough life by Ethiopian standards until one day she looked down her street and saw what others could not.

Haregewoin couldn't save everyone—a million people had died of AIDS in its first two decades in Ethiopia, and the hardest hit were the men and women (especially women) between fifteen and forty-nine years of age: a generation and a half of *parents*. Haregewoin Teferra was trying to harbor a few of the children left behind.[12]

Meanwhile, Greene's interests had been piqued when she heard Africa described as "a continent of orphans."

More than thirteen million children had been orphaned, twelve million of them in sub-Saharan Africa. Twenty-five percent of those lived in two countries: Nigeria and Ethiopia. In Ethiopia, 11 percent of all children were orphans.[13]

Her journey was not solely academic or journalistic, but personal: "I suddenly wondered, 'Can you adopt one of the African AIDS orphans?' The notion of adoption gave me a way in, a way to look behind the big numbers with all the zeros."[14]

Haregewoin sought housing for some of the children she simply did not have room for, only to learn that "Mother Teresa's [orphanage] was full."[15] Why had so many come to Haregewoin?

This slight gap in the impenetrable landscape—door after door closed to the afflicted, clergy preaching against them, their own families stonily denying them—had been discovered. Somehow the untouchables had found this woman who did not shriek insults, throw rocks, or shake a broom at them before slamming the door in their faces. Now they rode by bus or by donkey, they hiked or they limped, toward the brick house of Haregewoin Teferra, in a rickety hillside neighborhood of Addis Ababa.[16]

Greene raises the question in her book: "So how does it happen that—while most people instinctively try to save themselves and their families from a catastrophe—a few slow down, look back, and suddenly reach out to strangers? Instead of fleeing in the opposite direction, a few wade into the rising waters to try to yank the drowning onto higher land."[17] As Christians considering such a perspective, we must ask ourselves, could we not be involved in some way? Should we not be involved? The need is overwhelming, dizzying.

Some will make eloquent arguments about how adopting children from poorer countries or across cultural boundaries is a kind of theft, or a cultural violation, or some other monstrous intrusion. Each individual child would have a different perspective:

In the epoch of the HIV/AIDS pandemic, a few families from foreign countries were throwing lifelines to individual children. The life-changing opportunity was not without a price, which the Ethiopian government weighed carefully: the adopted children would lose their country, people, faith, language, culture, and history. A child could end up the sole Ethiopian for hundreds of miles; another, the only child of color in his or her school. But the adopted child would gain the one thing on earth arguably worth more than a homeland: family. While most African nations did not turn to intercountry adoption as an option for orphaned children, Ethiopian officials decided that for the infinitesimal minority of African orphans who could be raised by foreign parents, the trade-off was worthwhile and they would not block their path.

In 2005, Ethiopia had 1,563,000 AIDS orphans, the second-highest concentration of such children in the world; and 4,414,000 orphans from all causes, the second-highest number in Africa. Out of all these children, 1,400 departed for new families abroad that year.[18]

An infinitesimally small proportion of Ethiopia's children were in this way given new lives filled with possibilities. Greene summarizes the reality in this way: "For most of Africa's ten million, fifteen million, twenty million orphans, no one is getting a room ready. No one will come."[19]

ADOPTION AND EVANGELISM

Perhaps not surprisingly, in every evangelical church you will hear the topic of evangelism broached. Very often, it is presented in such a way that most of the congregation will feel a twinge of guilt ("I should do more; I should be bolder"). Adoption is the easiest form of evangelism imaginable. For years you will have the opportunity to pour your life into the life of another person in the quietude of your own home. Opportunities will arise naturally. You will be able to live out the ancient decrees as you seek to pass on the truths of our God:

> Impress them on your children. Talk about them when you sit at home and when you walk along the road, when you lie down and when you get up. Tie them as symbols on your hands and bind them on your foreheads. Write them on the doorframes of your houses and on your gates. (Deuteronomy 6:7-8)

I am a light-skinned Hispanic man with an African American son. My youngest son, Caleb, is adopted. In the first eleven years of his life, I can only recall two instances where anyone expressed something negative about a black son living in what they assume to be a white home. Hundreds of people, meanwhile, have been encouraging, quite often saying, "What a blessing you are to that child." In reality, we have never seen it this way. Instead, each day Caleb has been in our home has been a source of unending blessing to us. We may have sought to be a blessing, but one simply cannot outgive God: "Whoever sows generously will also reap generously" (2 Corinthians 9:6).

FOR FURTHER REFLECTION

Investigate how one adopts a child in the state or country you live in. It is amazing to see how the rules differ from place to place. Become an expert in how things take place in your area and seek to help others understand.

Someone with technical expertise could create a website or similar resource that makes this process easier. Is there something you can do to help make such a dream a reality?

13

Become a Foster Parent

*Whoever welcomes one of these little children
in my name welcomes me; and whoever
welcomes me does not welcome me
but the one who sent me.*

MARK 9:37

MANY COLLEGES ASSIGN A BOOK to incoming freshmen to read during the summer. The book is chosen, after much discussion, to introduce a complex and challenging topic and to serve as a theme for ongoing campus conversations. One popular selection in recent years has been New York Times best-seller *The Glass Castle*, by Jeannette Walls.

In *The Glass Castle* Walls describes growing up with three siblings in the Southwest and in a West Virginia mining town. The product of highly intellectual but highly unstable parents, she and her siblings slipped through the cracks of the child welfare system. Walls developed resourcefulness and courage, however, eventually striking out at the age of sixteen to New York City. She enrolled in Barnard College and eventually became a columnist and television personality. She has told her story through television and radio and makes public appearances all around the country. It's an inspiring story of surviving parental neglect and finding the resources she needed, despite the odds and the barriers. And yet the more common story is not one of flourishing but one of need.

In 1909 President Teddy Roosevelt sponsored the first White House Conference on the Care of Dependent Children to address the problem of child neglect.[1] One hundred years later, the problem looms even larger. Children end up in foster care because they cannot be cared for at home. Frequently, a crisis precipitates this outcome. A mother is discovered to be on drugs; a father has committed a crime and is now in jail; parents are homeless or perhaps in a home environment that is not fit for children. In such cases, the children are removed, and an effort is made to arrange transitional and temporary residence in a safe home. Most of the time, the children do not return to their original homes.

Children who end up in foster care have several strikes against them. Consider this case study:

The referral was a fairly routine assessment of a 16-month-old child, Jason. The child's family had become known to child welfare authorities 5 months earlier when a pediatrician identified malnutrition in the infant and his 3-year-old sister. The family was receiving in-home child welfare services. The social worker providing the in-home care was concerned about Jason's small size and apparently delayed development. She also worried about the lack of stimulation in the home. Because of these concerns, the social worker scheduled an appointment for a multidisciplinary assessment. When the family arrived for the developmental evaluation, the receptionist thought they had come in on the wrong date for their appointment because she expected to see a 16-month-old toddler and instead observed the father carrying what appeared to be an infant. In fact, he was carrying his 16-month-old son who was only dressed in a light, soiled, cotton nightgown, with no shoes, socks, gloves, or hat. The child's hands and feet were mottled from the cold. He was dirty and smelled of urine. . . . The results of the assessment indicated that Jason was not only the size of a 6-month-old but also had commensurate speech-language and gross motor skills. His cognitive functioning appeared to be at a 4-month level. In addition to this global developmental delay, a physical examination indicated that Jason had severe diaper rash, an ear infection, and severe hypotonia (low muscle tone). The developmental team filed an official child neglect report.[2]

Foster parents must be prepared for all kinds of trouble, starting with physical deficits. Visits to doctors, therapists, specialists—these are common starting points. Children who are products of neglect have a lot of catching up to do. One study evaluating the development of more than three hundred infants and toddlers who were connected to a child welfare agency indicated that 25 percent of the children had significant motor delays.[3]

Consider another case:

Erica was clinging to her mother, crying mournfully. Even when encouraged to comfort her 11-month-old daughter, Ms. Daniels seemed uncomfortable doing so and was unable to soothe her. Erica was the third child born to this mother who had been a victim of abuse and neglect herself. She had been incarcerated for the death of her first baby. Her second child had disabilities as a result of shaken baby syndrome. Although the child welfare authorities tried to remove Erica at birth from Ms. Daniels's care, a family court judge ruled that Erica should remain with her mother with some supportive services provided to them in their home. To monitor Erica's development, the child welfare worker arranged for an evaluation by a transdisciplinary team. The speech-language pathologist on the team informally interviewed Ms. Daniels to get a sense of Erica's speech-language development. The speech-language pathologist asked Ms. Daniels: "When you speak to your baby, does she look at your face?" Her response, "I never talk to my baby," was a major concern to the team.[4]

Longitudinal studies indicate that children from economically disadvantaged homes often have impoverished language skills. Growing up in homes that do not provide ready access to reading material, children are at a disadvantage when it comes to vocabulary and reading readiness. Once they hit preschool, they are forced to play catch-up. And school expectations just keep accelerating. If the child is older, say in middle or high school, the marks are there for life.

Typically the process of removal begins with a call. Somebody notices that things don't look quite right. The neighbor in the apartment building calls Social Services. A social worker shows up and assesses the situation. If the situation seems to be critical, the social worker petitions the court for a removal order. A policeman enters the home and removes the child. These scenes stay imprinted in the child's memory for life. The child sent to foster care feels indelibly "different."

The psychological effects of moving from one foster home to the next are difficult to overcome. And foster care has an expiration date. Each year, "between 18,500 and 25,000 teenagers 'age out' of foster care by virtue of reaching the age at which their legal right to foster care ends."[5] Though laws vary from state to state, in most cases the aging out occurs at 18. Thanks to the work of Senator John H. Chafee, a champion of children's issues, Congress approved in 1999 the Foster Care Independence Act, which increased federal funding and extended eligibility from age fourteen to age twenty-one.[6]

Martha Shirk and Gary Stangler note, however, that "despite the Chafee Act, many youth in care are still being sent out into the world with little more than a list of apartment rental agencies, a gift certificate to Wal-Mart, a bag full of manufacturer's samples, perhaps a cooking pot, maybe a mattress."[7] We know from personal experience that many eighteen-year-olds—like our own children, perhaps—are not sufficiently mature to be successful at independent living. Many have not yet developed the skills that they will need as adults. Transportation may very well be a challenge. At eighteen, what are the odds that most would make it in the job market?

There is a desperate need for a supportive network to help these young people transition to independence. But taking on the role of foster parent is a daunting prospect. The foster parent may need to be prepared to deal with all kinds of collateral damage. Physical damage. Emotional damage. Foster children can have a hard shell. They may have their guard up. Parenting these children may not be a warm, fuzzy experience.

Jesus spent time with children. They climbed on his lap and talked to him. Surely, in that group were some youngsters who knew trouble. Jesus was prepared to minister to them all. Foster parenting is a big commitment, but big commitments bring big rewards.

FOR FURTHER REFLECTION

While all of the topics in this book require thought, research and prayerful reflection, foster care is a domain that cannot be entered lightly. Because the challenge is severe, though, the need for Christian involvement is even more important. Consider taking the first steps that might allow you to serve in this vital way.

14

Fight Child Abuse

*If anyone causes one of these little ones who
believe in me to sin, it would be better
for him to have a large millstone hung
around his neck and to be drowned
in the depths of the sea.*

MATTHEW 18:6

ALL PEOPLE HAVE BASIC NEEDS, and these needs have different levels of intensity. The first level of Maslow's hierarchy of human needs involves physical necessities like food, clothing and shelter. The second level consists of needs for safety and security. The third level points to the need for love, belonging and a sense of being valued. The fourth level focuses on self-esteem and the fifth on the ultimate need: self-actualization. Child abuse cuts across all of these levels of need.

Child abuse can take the form of deprivation, as children are denied food, adequate clothing and adequate shelter. It can mean putting the child in an environment that is not safe, where there are various threats of harm. It can mean sexual abuse, emotional mistreatment, intimidation or manipulation. No matter what form it takes, child abuse ravages the child's sense of self and leaves permanent scars, visible or invisible.

Barbara Lowenthal reports that the rate of child maltreatment has been increasing at a rate of approximately 10 percent each year since 1976.[1] These numbers may very well be underestimated, since much abuse goes unreported. Lowenthal cites a report by the U.S. Advisory Board on Child Abuse and Neglect, which called child abuse "a national emergency" for the following reasons:

- Every year thousands of children in the United States are victims of violence, neglect, abandonment, emotional abuse and even torture.

- The current system has failed to prevent this maltreatment.

- That failure results in remedial programs that cost millions of dollars every year.[2]

Grotesque examples exist beyond the borders of the United States as well: child soldiers, victims of human trafficking and the like.

Professionals have identified a host of risk factors for abuse. Cynthia Crosson-Tower observes that child abuse "does not happen in a vacuum."[3] In some cases, there are difficulties with attachment; mothers who are suffering from postpartum depression or who simply do not have the emotional energy to give to their infants may ignore and neglect them. Children who are in a home where there is substance abuse or domestic violence are at risk for abuse. A battered woman may project "her own self-loathing and hatred onto the child."[4] Special-needs children, who present particular demands on caregivers, are potential targets for mistreatment.

Child abuse often surfaces in a public space as children bring signs of abuse to school. Kenneth Lau, Kathryn Krase and Richard Morse include a long list of signs of physical abuse, including head injuries, fractures, burns, bruises, welts, lacerations and bite marks. They also point out behavioral signs, such as social anxiety, aggression and bullying, chronic running away, fear of going home, self-blame, hiding injuries, depression and suicide attempts.[5] And then there's the nightmare of sexual abuse.

Parenting is not easy or natural to many; having to tend to the needs of a child can heighten the stresses that are already present in the home. Poverty, substance abuse, mental illness—all can increase the likelihood of abuse. Cynthia Crosson-Tower cites the work of Dr. Ray Helfer, who described abusive parents as those who are not prepared to become parents themselves. According to Helfer, they have not learned the five vital lessons of parenting:

- Abusive parents have not learned appropriate ways to have their needs met.

- Abusive parents have not learned the difference between feelings and actions.

- Abusive parents have not learned to make decisions.

- Abusive parents have not learned that they are responsible for their own actions.

- Abusive parents have not learned to delay gratification.[6]

The abusive parent is not always easy to spot. She can look like our next-door neighbor. Consider this example:

Libby Carter was a neat, well-dressed young woman whose house appeared immaculate—to the few who had seen it. Libby, her husband, and two children had recently moved and she reported knowing few people. Deeper exploration of Libby's family background would have revealed that she had married young and had had an extremely difficult time in her pregnancies, especially with Tommy, her first child. As a baby, Tommy had been colicky and difficult, and Libby, an only child, had felt at a loss to know what to do. Her husband, Mike, a hard-working, conservative man, expected her to know what to do. He often brought work home and was annoyed when Tommy's crying made it difficult to concentrate.

In addition, the couple never seemed to be able to make ends meet which caused a great deal of friction between them. This may not seem to be an unusual scenario in an age of unpredictable economy and increased mobility. However, Libby Carter was brought to the attention of the local protective agency because five-year-old Tommy repeatedly came to school with unexplained bruises.[7]

For more than fifty years, child advocates have been working on prevention efforts. The promotion of awareness is one important way to reduce abuse. Federally mandated laws such as the Child Abuse Prevention and Treatment Act of 1974 have made funding available to establish prevention programs. Sensational cases of abuse are regularly publicized by the media, thereby heightening general public awareness. For more than twenty years, educators have been integrating material on abuse into the classroom experience. These programs seem to help, but it takes a broader strategy to get at the heart of the problem

Cynthia Crosson-Tower suggests that both schools and communities need to be involved in a set of infused strategies:

- By providing life skills training
- By aiding in the preparation for parenthood
- By sponsoring self-protection training
- By providing educational services for the community
- By aiding in the help given to at-risk families

Common strategies involve workshops for parents, age-appropriate materials integrated into the classroom and community service projects that provide support for mothers, many of whom are barely out of high school.[8] Crosson-Tower also defines some of the common characteristics of abuse victims, who may have

- poor self-image
- unattended educational and medical needs
- hampered development emotionally, physically, or sexually

They may need

- individual attention
- to express frustration and anger
- to succeed—to do something right
- to know that they have rights too

Teachers and social workers will need to take into account all of these factors as they work with abused children.[9]

In decades of sermons and Sunday school lessons, I cannot recall the topic of child abuse being broached. Handbooks and manuals all offer helpful and important information about how to address the physical and emotional dimensions of abuse; it is harder to locate material that includes spiritual dimensions.

In the New Testament, we see Jesus surrounding himself with children:

> People were bringing little children to Jesus to have him touch them, but the disciples rebuked them. When Jesus saw this, he was indignant. He said to them, "Let the little children come to me, and do not hinder them, for the kingdom of God belongs to such as these." (Mark 10:13-14)

Jesus surrounded himself with broken people—the lame, the blind, the deaf. It is likely that in that throng of children, some were mistreated. Neglected. Maybe abused. Jesus went out of his way to seek out the company of children. In the passage above, he is surely advocating for them, chiding his disciples for neglecting them. His comment—the kingdom of God belongs to such as these—affirms the value of children, who were made in the image of God.

Committing ourselves to child advocacy is a worthy calling. We need social workers, lawyers, teachers and legislators to dedicate themselves to tackling this heartbreaking problem. Communities need to provide resources to struggling parents. Schools need to offer instruction and a safe haven for children who have nowhere else to turn. We all should educate ourselves about this issue and remain alert to the signs of abuse. And we should be willing to intervene if we see a child in trouble.

FOR FURTHER REFLECTION

In your church, seek to raise awareness of the reality of child abuse. Since the church has been largely silent on this horrid problem, discuss with pastors and other leaders the necessity of clear communication—and ministry.

15

Fight Pornography

*Those who belong to Christ Jesus have crucified the
sinful nature with its passions and desires.
Since we live by the Spirit, let us
keep in step with the Spirit.*

GALATIANS 5:24-25

ANYONE WHO ATTEMPTS TO BROACH the topic of pornography must begin by acknowledging that it is a fraught subject, awkward, uncomfortable, one we might well be tempted to keep private.

And pornography is certainly not new. Archaeologists have unearthed evidence of pornography in ancient cultures, including Greece and Rome. The Middle Ages produced it. It continued to be popular during the Renaissance and into the seventeenth and eighteenth centuries. The Victorian era saw the rise of pornography as an industry—coinciding with the introduction of the camera. Today it's firmly entrenched, and apparently here to stay. Billions of dollars are spent every year on magazines and movies. Porn is as near as your computer or smart phone. There's pornography for every taste. No matter what you like, the images are there.

In some ways, the use of pornography appears to be a fairly harmless practice, a victimless recreation (assuming one ignores

Jesus' words in the Sermon on the Mount: "But I tell you that anyone who looks at a woman lustfully has already committed adultery with her in his heart" [Matthew 5:28]). After all, nothing "real" happens. A man or woman who indulges in pornography may safely maintain their public fidelity to their spouse, as well as their reputation. Some feminists have even argued that women should have free reign in their choices, including the free choice to deploy their bodies for pornographic purposes.

Jacques Lacan introduced the term *gaze* to the arena of psychology. Gaze describes the state of recognizing that one is a visible object. Lacan identified this recognition as the mirror stage, when a child becomes aware of his/her personal appearance.[1] This term has been put to use by art critics and film critics alike, who apply the term "the male gaze" to art that puts the audience into the perspective of a heterosexual male. Consequently even women often look at themselves through the eyes of men, as Laura Mulvey explains in a classic essay called "Visual Pleasure and Narrative Cinema."[2]

The sexualizing male gaze is prevalent in American culture and, increasingly, around the world. Abercrombie and Fitch ads, Victoria's Secret window displays, late-night commercials for chat lines and myriad online sources—all place women in provocative poses for the enjoyment of the male spectator. Little girls as young as six or seven begin to think of themselves as sex objects, with a goal of dressing to look hot. Schoolgirls wear outfits that evoke the world of nightclubs. Is anyone who feels bothered by these displays just old-fashioned? Sexually repressed?[3]

Nevertheless, pornography is at the least a murky enterprise. Links between pornography and poverty, exploitation, domestic abuse, child abuse, violence and drug addiction abound. Sexual tourism, child pornography and other horrors are fueled by the desires that pornography inspires. The correlation between human trafficking and sexual exploitation of every kind is very high. As marijuana can be touted as a gateway drug to more severe addictions, so also pornography is a kind of gateway drug to every kind of sexual deviance.

We could easily go to the Scriptures and cite verses warning us against lust, concupiscence and uncleanness (e.g., 1 Thessalonians 4:5-7). But instead, let's go to a book of the Bible that is often neglected: the Song of Songs. I've spent a lifetime in church, and while my experience may be unique, I don't recall a single sermon focused on this book. When it is mentioned, it's often presented as an extended allegory about Christ's relationship with his bride, the church. Readers who are generally prone to literal interpretations in this case run from the story that is told: an intensely erotic account of a courtship and marriage.

The book unfolds as an series of love lyrics, alternating between the perspective of the woman (the Shulamite maiden) and the perspective of the man (Solomon). The imagery is sensual, tactile, evoking the sights, smells and tastes of the human lovers. The lovers speak tenderly to each other: "How beautiful you are, my darling! Oh, how beautiful! Your eyes are doves" (1:15). The maiden responds, mirroring his words of love, "How handsome you are, my lover! Oh, how charming! And our bed is verdant" (1:16). There is perfume. There is gazing. The lovers enjoy the delights of human love as they interact lovingly with one another. In Jewish culture, the Songs are used as part of the wedding liturgy. Surely this book is in the Bible for an important reason: to show us God's affirmation of sexual experience within the context of marriage.

Contrast this picture of erotic enjoyment with what happens with pornography. First, an inherently participatory experience, involving two living, breathing people, devolves into voyeurism. Second, the images that are standard in pornography are painfully artificial. An air-brushed woman is splayed across the page (or the screen) in unnatural, uncomfortable poses. Teetering on stilettos, her eyes might be gazing out provocatively at the spectator, or they might be gazing out vacantly into space. Who knows what she is thinking? Who cares? From the point of view of the male gazer, she is only a body. There is no engagement with the whole person. Her mind, her spirit—all irrelevant. She is positioned for one purpose only: to stimulate male desire. Ironically, there is no prospect of any satisfaction. *It's guaranteed to disappoint.* That's what keeps the customer coming back. So the quest continues as one image leads to another.

The problem with pornography is that it isn't sexual enough. It is one-dimensional, incomplete, empty. Meanwhile, a married man who indulges in pornography will surely bring unrealistic expectations back to his wife, and the disappointment will continue.

Pornography diminishes women—and men. This is a problem that should be attacked at its root, within the family. Husbands who want to honor and please their wives should eschew pornography. Women should hold high expectations of their husbands. Fathers should convey to their daughters their worth and value. Mothers should hold their sons to high standards of conduct and respect. Parents should set ground rules for how their children dress. Families should treat the treatment of sexuality on television as teachable moments. They should use the bad behavior of other people as opportunities to educate children on a positive, biblical sexuality. Parents should have conversations about sexuality with their children from an early age. These conversations may at times be uncomfortable, but the more uncomfortable they are, the more important they are.

Ironically, pornography doesn't take sex seriously enough. The Song of Solomon unapologetically portrays sex as a glorious gift, invented and given by God, to be reserved for the context of marriage. Used in this way, we are reminded by even our sexuality that we are formed in the image and likeness of God.

FOR FURTHER REFLECTION

One organization that unabashedly seeks to help those who are addicted to pornography, as well as its victims, is www.xxxchurch.com. Familiarize yourself with that site and take advantage of its services.

Consider ways by which this topic can be brought from out of dark alleys into the full light of day among your network of trusted friends, and determine how you can all help each other to resist the allure of pornography.

16

Support Women's Shelters

He will rescue them from oppression and violence,
for precious is their blood in his sight.

PSALM 72:14

The LORD works righteousness
and justice for all the oppressed.

PSALM 103:6

DOMESTIC VIOLENCE IS A GLOBAL PROBLEM. Spend a few moments on the Internet and you will find thousands statistics, legal cases and personal narratives documenting the ugly fact of domestic violence around the world. The National Organization for Women, government websites in all developed countries, the World Health Organization—all point to the magnitude and intransigence of domestic violence.

Nor is domestic violence a recent problem. Even the most basic familiarity with history, sociology and women's studies suggests that for much of human history, women have been subjected to what one organization calls the "hidden hurt" of abuse (www.hiddenhurt.co.uk). The problem is not circumscribed by class, race or socioeconomic status. It transcends all of these identifiers. The abused woman could be any woman anywhere.

Millions of women. Every year. A frequently cited statistic goes like this: one out of every four women will experience domestic violence in her lifetime, perpetrated by a family member, a boy-friend or a spouse. Emma's story. Kiara's story. Rachel's story. In many ways they are much the same story. The first slap. Broken ribs. Unexplained bruises. Trips to the emergency room. Promises that it will stop. And the cycle continues. Victims tend to come from abusive families.[1] Victimized women tend to produce daughters who, thinking that abuse is normal, settle into abusive relation-ships. Daughters might extrapolate abusiveness from their fathers (or their mothers' boyfriends, or whomever) to all men. Or they may come to assume that all relationships have an element of vio-lence in them, so that abuse becomes for them a normal facet of any relationship. Not to mention that boys experience the same dy-namics, normalizing abuse in relationships based on the behavior they observe between their parents.

If we want to make this personal, we might look at our particular social circles: if the statistics are accurate, we are very likely friends with not one *but several* victims of abuse. It could well be that our next-door neighbor, our best friend, our own sister may be strug-gling with this kind of humiliating and dehumanizing treatment. And the catastrophic effects of abuse do not stop with women. Often children are also involved.

What makes this social ill especially difficult to address is its hidden, shameful nature. Women who are victims of domestic abuse are famously prone to deny that they are victims and to defend their abusers. They are frequently marginal in multiple ways—perhaps lacking in work skills that would allow them to support themselves, perhaps involved in drug addiction, perhaps weighed down with child-rearing duties. Sometimes mental illness is at play. The psychology of abuse is such that the woman feels that she can't leave.

Because this problem is all around us, we might expect that the church would be taking it on. Surely pastors are in a position to hear of these cases and to do something about the tragedy of abuse. Ironically, however, domestic violence survivors relate that all too often appealing to the clergy for help is in vain. Like the Levite who walked right past the injured man, the pastor might very well prefer to look the other way. Worse, he might counsel battered women to stay the course.[2]

The work of tackling this issue has fallen to the professionals; sociologists have produced a whole body of literature documenting the problem of domestic violence. And they've done so in a way that is compelling enough to inspire a core of committed volunteers. If you are interested, there is most likely a venue in your area. As an example, InterAct is a private, nonprofit United Way agency whose mission is to provide support to victims and survivors of domestic violence and rape/sexual assault. InterAct draws on volunteers and community support, sponsoring charity balls, silent marches and holiday bazaars. InterAct and other similar organizations, however, are in no way affiliated with the church. We might wonder: why has the church steered away from this clear and pressing problem?

A few people—typically women—have carried the banner. Author and New Testament scholar Catherine Clark Kroeger created a foundation called Peace and Safety in the Christian Home. Kroeger's work, along with the work of sociologist Nancy Nason-Clark, is an example of the efforts of women to bring public attention to domestic violence.[3] Their efforts—and those of others like them—are noteworthy and have done some good. But they are not enough.

How would Jesus want us to respond to domestic violence? Are there principles we can infer from his interactions with women? Let us consider two examples: the Samaritan woman, and Mary Magdalene.

John 4:4-42 describes Jesus' encounter with a Samaritan woman. It is well known that in choosing to converse with a Samaritan, Jesus was crossing cultural boundaries. Jesus' willingness to interact with a woman, however, was equally shocking. Karen Thiessen notes that rabbinical thought was such that men were prohibited from speaking to women in public; Jewish literature "tended to characterize women as unclean sexual temptresses."[4] Within this context, Jesus speaks openly and fearlessly to a woman—and a woman with a murky past at that. The disciples marvel that he is engaged in conversation with this woman, who has had five husbands and is currently living with another man. When Jesus confronts her with the details of her messy personal life, he does so directly, without averting his eyes. Moreover, he makes of her a shocking request—to give him water—and goes on to offer her living water. To translate the scene into modern terms, Jesus is offering this damaged woman a new life. After her encounter with Jesus, the woman is changed forever.

Another telling example involves Jesus' interaction with Mary Magdalene, perhaps the most notorious woman in all of Scripture. Though scholars continue to debate the details of her life, Luke 8:2 states plainly that Jesus removed seven devils from her. Tradition depicts her as a prostitute; her penitence and transformation became the stuff of legend, art and film. In the nineteenth century, her name was associated with "Magdalene" houses, institutions for fallen women.

Mary Magdalene's appearances in the New Testament point to a recovered life. Clearly identified as among the women who had followed Jesus when he was in Galilee and who remained with him until his death, Mary Magdalene had a place in Jesus' inner circle. She is often identified as the unnamed woman who brings perfume and pours it on Jesus' head and washes his feet (Luke 7:37-38). In an similar scene in John 12, Mary is reproached by the disciples, but Jesus affirms her, declaring what she has done shall be a memorial to her. Luke 24 tells us that the resurrected Jesus appeared first to Mary Magdalene, who was given the glorious mission of taking the news to the disciples. A damaged woman. A shamed woman. This woman was chosen by the Savior for healing and for a new life. If, upon reflection, we take in the surprising reality that Jesus included a broken woman in his circle, offering her hope and restoration, we might also begin to think that his church should take a look at broken women and assist in their restoration.

Women's shelters routinely attain some visibility at Christmas. It is comparatively easy to purchase toiletries and leave them in a donations box. What we may be called upon to do, however, is to face this messy reality and to do so steadily. Not once a year, but every day, paying attention to the bruised women we are very likely seeing on the elevator, in the grocery store, in the classroom, maybe even in our pews. Women's shelters need volunteers. Jesus paid attention to broken women. So should we. And while we're at it, we would do well to point them to Jesus, in whom they will find their ultimate shelter.

FOR FURTHER REFLECTION

Research women's shelters in your area. Find a way to help.

17

Care for Widows

*Religion that God our Father accepts as pure and faultless is this:
to look after orphans and widows in their distress and
to keep oneself from being polluted by the world.*

JAMES 1:27

THERE ARE ALL KINDS OF EFFECTS associated with finding oneself left to stand alone. Grown children may be a helpful resource, but typically they have their own lives. They may not live close by. Widows—usually in the later decades of life—must rebuild their lives, all the while dealing with grief. Young widows may find themselves with children to raise alone.

Widowhood is a hot topic on Amazon.com. Anyone facing this kind of loss can find books galore, from *Widow: A Survival Guide for the First Year* and *A Widow's Story* to *Happily Even After: A Guide to Getting Through (and Beyond) the Grief of Widowhood*. Though the books attempt to explain what to expect during the mourning process, there is no single template for grief. Author Mary Jane Worden kept a journal of her first year without her husband and muses at the variety of feelings involved in grief. "One big component of the pain," she writes, "is fear—a fear that this experience of pain may not be momentary but might settle down on me as a permanent condition, an incurable disease, an overwhelming and unmoving cloud cover."[1]

Finances can be a concern. Widows quickly realize that they must learn to manage in straitened circumstances. Some have depended on their spouses to deal with the complexities of day-to-day operations. Perhaps they have never paid much attention to the details of filing taxes, monitoring interest rates or making wise investments. Now, under great duress, they must take care of these things. It can be overwhelming.

Home maintenance is another challenge. A widow may have to hire out basic maintenance for the first time. And there's lawn care. And car maintenance. All of these areas needing attention at the same time. Suddenly the widow must make all of the decisions and carry them out.

Then there are the social ramifications. It can be frightening to have to get around alone. People who are used to fitting into social structures as one-half of a couple now find themselves on the periphery, the proverbial third wheel. Generally, widows are accustomed to appearing in public with their spouses. Just going to church can become a daunting prospect. Sitting alone in a restaurant for the first time in decades may be so dispiriting that some widows just decide to stay home and eat alone—that is, if they're eating. Widows are in danger of losing weight, forgetting to eat, failing to seek medical help. Health can decline. They get depressed. They can't sleep. Loneliness becomes chronic. They might even lose their faith. Eugenia Price observed, "It just takes time even for God to get through our sorrow."[2]

Many widows find it helpful to join a group—a network for mutual support and commiseration. When these groups work well, widows form sustaining friendships and organize themselves for mutual caregiving, taking turns driving one another to the doctor, sitting with one another through surgeries, making meals for one another. They stand by each other as new crises or new causes for celebration emerge.

The Book of Ruth contains one of the most poignant accounts of widowhood in all of Scripture.

Now Elimelek, Naomi's husband, died, and she was left with her two sons. They married Moabite women, one named Orpah and the other Ruth. After they had lived there about ten years, both Mahlon and Kilion also died, and Naomi was left without her two sons and her husband.

When she heard in Moab that the LORD had come to the aid of his people by providing food for them, Naomi and her daughters-in-law prepared to return home from there. With her two daughters-in-law she left the place where she had been living and set out on the road that would take them back to the land of Judah.

Then Naomi said to her two daughters-in-law, "Go back, each of you, to your mother's home. May the LORD show kindness to you, as you have shown to your dead husbands and to me. May the LORD grant that each of you will find rest in the home of another husband."

Then she kissed them goodbye and they wept aloud and said to her, "We will go back with you to your people."

But Naomi said, "Return home, my daughters. Why would you come with me? Am I going to have any more sons, who could become your husbands? Return home, my daughters; I am too old to have another husband. Even if I thought there was still hope for me—even if I had a husband tonight and then gave birth to sons—would you wait until they grew up? Would you remain unmarried for them? No, my daughters. It is more bitter for me than for you, because the LORD's hand has turned against me!"

At this they wept aloud again. Then Orpah kissed her

mother-in-law goodbye, but Ruth clung to her.

"Look," said Naomi, "your sister-in-law is going back to her people and her gods. Go back with her."

But Ruth replied, "Don't urge me to leave you or to turn back from you. Where you go I will go, and where you stay I will stay. Your people will be my people and your God my God." (Ruth 1:3-16)

Naomi's experience is one of dislocation and double bereavement. A native of Bethlehem, Naomi relocates after her marriage to the country of Moab, leaving behind family and familiarity. When her husband dies, she must depend on her two sons, who have taken Moabite women as wives. When the sons die, she is left with her daughters-in-law, who join her in widowhood. Without minimizing the challenges faced by Naomi and her daughters-in-law, the biblical writer emphasizes the mutual support the women offer each other. So precarious is the plight of the widow that one of the Jewish laws makes provision for her: Deuteronomy 24:20 says, "When you beat the olives from your trees, do not go over the branches a second time. Leave what remains for the alien, the fatherless and the widow." Without such provision, widows would have had no guarantee of basic needs. Ruth's refusal to leave her mother-in-law, despite her youthful prospects of remarriage, underscores how alone and how dependent Naomi was in a world without many safety nets.

Even with modern safety nets, widowhood continues to be a major life challenge. Fortunately, churches have begun to offer help. James says that true religion involves caring for the widow (James 1:27); fortunately, widow care is available in many forms. Bible studies, ladies' lunches, bus trips—all can be useful as widows re-invent their lives. Today, widows can practice the same solidarity that we see in the book of Ruth.

If you would like to be involved in this kind of ministry, opportunities are not hard to find. If your particular church does not offer such a program, you might explore what the needs are and seek to create a support group.

Youth groups are always looking for service projects. Widows need their yards raked, their decks painted, their cars washed. This kind of intergenerational interaction is mutually instructive and satisfying. Young people get a glimpse of the daily realities that might befall their parents. Widows get the help they need, all the while perhaps making new friends and getting their spirits lifted.

Looking after the widows in our community is a potent reminder of the precariousness of our lives—and our need to model the care that James linked with religion that is alone acceptable before God.

FOR FURTHER REFLECTION

There is much counsel in Scripture relating to widows and our treatment of them. Take out a concordance, or use a website that allows you to search for terms. First Timothy 5, all too rarely considered, offers some particular insight.

Once your understanding of Scripture rises on this subject, it may be that you will better notice the people in your lives that need care.

18

Care for the Disabled

Then Jesus said to his host, "When you give a luncheon or dinner, do not invite your friends, your brothers or relatives, or your rich neighbors; if you do, they may invite you back and so you will be repaid. But when you give a banquet, invite the poor, the crippled, the lame, the blind, and you will be blessed. Although they cannot repay you, you will be repaid at the resurrection of the righteous."

LUKE 14:12-14

DISABILITY STUDIES IS A RELATIVELY NEW FIELD. In 1993 the Society for Disability Studies (SDS), an international nonprofit organization dedicated to the study of disability in social, cultural and political contexts, developed a definition of the field: disability studies "examines the policies and practices of all societies to understand the social, rather than the physical or psychological determinants of the experience of disability." Further, the goal of disability studies is to "disentangle impairments from the myths, ideology and stigma that influence social interaction and social policy." The scholarship issuing from this academic discipline "challenges the idea that the economic and social statuses and the assigned roles of people with disabilities are the inevitable outcomes of their condition."[1] SDS is committed to promoting greater awareness of the experiences of disabled people and to advocate for social change.

The Americans with Disabilities Act of 1990, a civil rights law that prohibits discrimination based on disability, was amended with changes effective January 1, 2009. It defines disability as "a physical or mental impairment that substantially limits a major life activity." Among other things, the act guarantees to students with documented disabilities access to education—and appropriate accommodations to level the playing field in academic settings.

The disabilities that are obvious to the eye are perhaps the easiest of all to deal with. After all, making changes in the environment is a well-defined task. Let's say, for example, that a student has mobility challenges. Schools are required by law to provide equal access within the classroom. This access might mean ramps and elevators. If the school building is old and lacks an elevator, it may mean rearranging classes so that they are all on the first floor. It may mean providing larger desks, or adjusting the height of desks. It might mean widening aisles in computer labs. Students whose egress depends on wheelchairs may need a button to open doors. Students who are visually impaired may need note-takers or special equipment that would allow them to tape lectures. Hearing-impaired students may need an interpreter. Visually impaired students would have other needs. These kinds of needs are quite straightforward, the solutions easily procurable.

Some disabilities are less visible, however. It is not unusual for college freshmen to bring in accommodations letters with a diagnosis of ADD (Attention Deficit Disorder), ADHD (Attention Deficit Hyperactivity Disorder), anxiety disorders or panic disorders. These disabilities are harder to deal with since they are unpredictable and intransigent. Students with ADHD or ADD sometimes have a record of academic difficulty. They know that they are going to have trouble on tests. They may have developed personal strategies for academic success. They may have difficulty focusing. They may miss important elements in a set of directions. They may not be able to sustain eye contact. Their writing may be all over the board; each paragraph containing a set of unrelated ideas. Students with anxiety disorders or panic disorders are prone to miss class or to have difficulties with deadlines. Often the pressure of a due date triggers an episode. These bouts are frequently accompanied by embarrassment, and sometimes students are reluctant to seek help to start with or are reluctant to disclose the nature of their problem. For this kind of student, even going to a counseling center or to disabilities services is a major hurdle. Students with these complex challenges need a multipronged approach and much support as they work through their difficulties.

Parents can help their children get the help they need by encouraging them to self-identify. It is not unusual for a student who has had a bad semester to request a conference with a teacher or adviser. If the semester has been bad enough, sometimes a parent asks to be part of the conference. The parent may be helpful in filling in the context of the child's performance in school—from kindergarten forward. As Janice McLaughlin and Dan Goodley note,

> Part of the productive identities of parents is to be a seeker of knowledge and acquirer of expertise. Knowledge and expertise are important parts of what they do (and who they are as caring and activist parents). They draw on a range of sources of knowledge and expertise, which helps them become partners with service providers, where recognition of their expertise is acknowledged, appreciated, and used in the support of the child.[2]

Education is a key step: parents who are well informed are more likely to be effective advocates for their children. Ultimately, however, the goal is for the child to be his or her own best advocate.

School systems are becoming better at training and resource

management, but the media makes sure we hear the horror stories—needs that were not addressed, unconscionable delays in providing services, funding deficits. While our school system pays lip service to equal opportunity, we know there are too many cases where children slip through the cracks.

How can we help? Parents can educate themselves in order to support their children with disabilities. But it is the responsibility of all of us to be sensitive to the issue of disability.

School counselors routinely talk to kids about sensitive topics. One common strategy that guidance counselors use to explain autism involves showing pictures of faces and asking kids to "read" the emotions on each face. A counselor will explain that some kids can't tell what people were feeling from their faces. These early lessons are appropriate in sensitizing children to what their peers may be facing—and in teaching them how to respond appropriately.

Advocacy work is another venue. Trained experts are needed. We need medical understanding. We need folks with training in social work, in psychology, in education. We need caring and trained teachers. We need people with strong communication and writing skills to help articulate the issues and the needs. It is so easy to stop with the physical and academic needs of the disabled. But there are spiritual needs as well. Care for the disabled takes many forms. There is a way for you to be involved.

Mark Pinsky, in an article titled "Churches Mustn't Neglect the Disabled," offers some important nuance to the complexity of the problem:

> In the Gospel of Luke, early Christians are urged to "invite the poor, the crippled, the lame, the blind" (14:13) to their gatherings. But how far can—or should—modern religious congregations go to accommodate people with physical or intellectual disabilities?

With the Baby Boom generation about to age into infirmity, and wounded war veterans returning from Iraq and Afghanistan in growing numbers, the issue of worshippers with disabilities will very soon overwhelm ethical and theological abstraction.

But half the congregations in the USA have fewer than 100 members—many in small towns and rural areas—which means the financial cost of adjusting their structures, Sunday schools and weekly services for one or two hearing-impaired or autistic or wheelchair using members can be a challenge. Building a ramp out of plywood is one thing; installing an elevator is quite another.[3]

For all of the modern church's emphasis to attract new members, human beings who are afflicted in a wide range of different ways are marginalized by society, and the church has not been consistently engaged in reaching out to these people in our communities. Will the next generation be able to note a difference in how your church is working in this area? We live in the hope that the prophet expresses: "In a very short time, will not Lebanon be turned into a fertile field and the fertile field seem like a forest? In that day the deaf will hear the words of the scroll, and out of gloom and darkness the eyes of the blind will see. Once more the humble will rejoice in the LORD; the needy will rejoice in the Holy One of Israel" (Isaiah 29:17-19).

FOR FURTHER REFLECTION

Imagine you lived in a poor country and were unable to walk. Imagine how you might live with blindness, or deafness, or another serious issue to contend with.

Organize a group to send a mission trip into a region that needs help working with the disabled.

19

Give Hospice Care

The man who was dying blessed me.

JOB 29:13

*This chapter was written by a colleague
as a reflection on the death of a parent.*

WHEN A CLASSMATE OF MY SON lost his father in fourth grade, the kids were ushered into a room with a guidance counselor to be instructed on what to say to a person who has lost a loved one. My son, eager to process the new information, told me all about it on the car ride home. "You should *not* say he's in a better place," my son said. "It's also not a good idea to say that you know how he feels. Because you don't."

I seemed to run into that child every time I visited my son's school. I would see teachers walking by and putting a hand on the child's shoulder. They didn't seem to be saying much.

We are at a loss in the face of death. A quick search on Amazon using the words "death and dying" yields 11,799 results. There are books galore: *You or a Loved One Dying? Be Not Afraid. Reflections: A Guide to End of Life Issues for You and Your Family. What Dying People*

Want: Practical Wisdom for the End of Life. The experts instruct us on how to talk to those who are nearing the end and those who are living with the prospect of loss. We have "issues" with death.

Hospice care emerged in the United Kingdom in the 1960s and in the United States in the 1970s.[1] The hospice movement has as one of its aims the goal of caring for the dying person's emotional and spiritual needs. Prior to that, treatment of dying patients was about illness management. The emergence of hospice care thus reflected a shift in the health care system away from treating a disease to treating the whole person.

I lost my mother four years ago. She had been declining for two years, was on oxygen twenty-four hours a day, and was in a wheelchair. She could transfer from the wheelchair to the bed with help. A fall and a crisis brought her to the hospital, where the ER doctor steered us toward intubation, declaring that it was what she would do for her own mother. My father, sister and I consented to the treatment.

My mother's CO_2 levels were so high that she was combative, accusing the medical staff of mistreating her. Perhaps she was right. A day later found her in intensive care, strapped to a machine, with the saddest eyes I had ever seen. Pleading eyes. She made it clear that she wanted a piece of paper. In scraggly letters she wrote the word *hell*. Later, after the ventilator was removed, she whispered, "Never again."

I had to ask: "No matter what?"

She answered, "No matter what."

Looking back, I know that we were fortunate to know exactly what our mother wanted. Families who have not had that conversation with their dying loved ones must agonize about their options. CPR? DNR? Life on a ventilator? Quantity or quality of life?

I recall the sweetness of my last conversations with my mother—conversations we would not have otherwise had. I recall the kindnesses of doctors. My mother was very near the end when the palliative care doctor called us, not once but repeatedly. I kept missing her calls. Or I just wouldn't return them. One day, maybe a week into my mother's hospitalization, I finally had a conversation with her. She arranged a private meeting with me, my father, my mother and my sister. She asked us what we wanted. When we reached the edge of a key question—whether to take my mother home—she said, ever so gently, "You know she's not going home." She then told us that there was a hospice floor and that my mother could be moved there. It was a tremendous relief to know about that option, though my mother never made it to that floor. I can still see the tender face of that palliative care doctor. I received a handwritten note from her several weeks after my mother passed. She knew exactly what was needed in our situation.

Hospice volunteers are regularly mentioned in obituary notices, for good reason. They bring comfort to the dying and the grieving. Dealing with death—whether our own or anybody else's—shakes us. Facing mortality is perhaps the hardest thing we ever do. It's what Jesus did when he assumed human form, consenting to die. Jesus did not avoid the dying. He became one of them.

The story of Lazarus is useful as we seek to understand what the Bible has to say about responding to death. The outlines of the story are familiar. Lazarus, brother of Mary and Martha, fell ill, and the sisters sent word to Jesus, who delayed for two more days. By the time Jesus arrived, Lazarus had been dead for four days. When Jesus arrived, Martha, rushing out to greet him, said, "If you had been here, my brother would not have died" (John 11:21). Mary, having stayed in the house with her friends, learned that Jesus had come and fell at his feet, saying the very same thing: "Lord, if you had been here, my brother would not have died" (John 11:32). If Jesus said comforting words to the sisters, they are not recorded.

Jesus, seeing Mary weeping, "was deeply moved in spirit and troubled" (John 11:33). As he learned where Lazarus was buried, we read one of the most famous verses in the New Testament: "Jesus wept" (John 11:35). Instead of healing Lazarus from afar, a thing he surely could have done, Jesus let his dear friend die. *And then he grieved.* Knowing he would resurrect Lazarus, Jesus nevertheless opened himself to the entire range of human loss and grief, putting himself into the middle of life's most painful experience: death.

And of course, the story doesn't end there. Jesus commanded that the stone covering the grave be moved.

Martha, horrified, reminded Jesus of the smell of death—a smell that Jesus made no effort to avoid. Jesus called Lazarus out of the grave and resurrected him, having explained that those who witnessed this would "see the glory of God" (John 11:40).

Jesus went about the dying. He had friends and experienced bereavement. He did not protect himself, nor did he protect others from the experience of death. He taught us that, viewed rightly, death could become a vehicle for the "glory of God."

Those of us who have sat in hospital rooms—as we all surely will—know the feelings of anxiety and sadness that the prospect of death brings. But we also know the unexpected rewards that going through such an experience can confer. It is in those moments when we are most vulnerable—whether as patient or loved one— that we are also the most open to the essential lessons of faith. Illness and death can thus be pathways. In his bestseller *The Care of the Soul*, Thomas Moore writes,

> The point is not to understand the cause of the disease and
> then solve the problem, but to get close enough to the disease
> to restore the particular religious connection with life at
> which it hints. . . . In a very real sense, we do not cure diseases,
> they cure us, by restoring our religious participation in life.[2]

I remember one morning, very early, while my mother was in hospice. A lovely young Indian doctor entered her room. She checked the settings on my mother's medical equipment and then lingered by her bed, touching her. I was on the cot; thinking me asleep, she tiptoed past me, and as she passed, she pulled the blanket over my feet.

In moments like those, with death imminent, we can know the glory of God.

FOR FURTHER REFLECTION

Hospice care is a difficult calling. Not everyone can do this work. But some can. If you have a vocation for sitting with the dying, for sitting with the family, you are doing God's work and are having a hand in bringing about the glory of God.

20

Fight for Human Rights

You rescue the poor from those too strong for them,
the poor and needy from those who rob them.

PSALM 35:10

Sing to the LORD! Give praise to the LORD!
He rescues the life of the needy
from the hands of the wicked.

JEREMIAH 20:13

NUMBED. IN THE COURSE OF HUMAN HISTORY, no age is as keenly aware of so many heartbreaking things (we are, perhaps, still ignorant of others). We grow inured to images of those who are hurting around the world: brown and tan and yellow babies, wrinkled men and women, disconsolate souls trudging through life looking for firewood or a care package or a safe haven. Dirty people whose reality we cannot smell but can sense at a distance. Such images are overwhelming, and we move on. Pinterest beckons.

In America, we have come to view the Declaration of Independence to be almost on par with Scripture: "We hold these truths to

be self-evident, that all men are created equal, that they are en-
dowed by their Creator with certain unalienable Rights, that among
these are Life, Liberty and the pursuit of Happiness." Who among
us would not want to see equality, life, liberty and happiness extended to everyone? But these are by no means universal marks.

Consider the example of just one region, and think about what
you might do to address these extraordinary difficulties:

> In Sub-Saharan Africa, malaria kills nearly one million people
> each year, and many deaths go unrecorded in rural areas.
> Moreover, this figure is still rising. Chad's maternal mortality
> rates are the world's third highest, and more than 80 percent
> of the women face female circumcision. And each year, as the
> rainy season ends, rebels are on the move from the east, where
> tens of thousands of refugees from the even more beleaguered
> Darfur region of Sudan and the Central African Republic lan-
> guish in overcrowded refugee camps.[1]

Equality? Hardly. Gender and racial lines sharply divide the
privileged and underprivileged. Life? Liberty? Happiness? For
many these must seem like pipe dreams. The concern is simple:
how can we make it through this day alive?

We look to governments and the United Nations to make an
impact in such cases, but time and again we have seen how pouring
even billions of dollars into a country does not guarantee progress
and in fact may bring about unintended consequences.[2] We might
be tempted to dismiss worldwide problems associated with human
rights as complex, enormous and intractable. We might let ourselves off the hook by remembering what Jesus said: "The poor you
will always have with you" (Matthew 26:11). But pause long
enough to ask the most important question: did Jesus call us to
tackle only the manageable problems?

We quote potent verses to one another quite often:

- "I tell you the truth, if you have faith as small as a mustard seed, you can say to this mountain, 'Move from here to there' and it will move. Nothing will be impossible for you" (Matthew 17:20).

- "I tell you the truth, anyone who has faith in me will do what I have been doing. He will do even greater things than these, because I am going to the Father. And I will do whatever you ask in my name, so that the Son may bring glory to the Father. You may ask me for anything in my name, and I will do it" (John 14:12-14).

- "Now to him who is able to do immeasurably more than all we ask or imagine, according to his power that is at work within us, to him be glory in the church and in Christ Jesus throughout all generations, for ever and ever! Amen" (Ephesians 3:20-21).

There are countless such passages in Scripture, along with countless flesh-and-blood examples of men and women who, by faith, conquered in the midst of the most refractory trials. We celebrate the victory of Gideon, for example, as he leads a mere three hundred unlikely soldiers in a plan of attack. We pass such verses around like sugar pills as we pat one another on the head in dealing with this week's little trial. Meanwhile, others around the world know real suffering. May God forgive us for spouting platitudes.

James Orbinski is an ordinary man who sought to make a positive difference in the lives of people. Often this impulse took him into the midst of the world's worst war zones. This exchange he had with another worker is telling:

> "Why did you stay?" I asked. "Because it was possible to do something, even something small that helped," Michel answered immediately. He paused and then said, "Once you're there, there is no other choice." "I know exactly what you mean," I replied.[3]

Orbinksi's reflections appear to be largely secular in their orientation, but a few spiritual notions peek through nevertheless:

The priest stayed with us for about five days. He never ate a full meal, only a few mouthfuls at each sitting. Even as he walked, he mumbled constantly, praying, looking down to something on the floor. When he sat, he pulled at his fingers, and his toes opened and closed as if he was trying to scratch against the soles of his sandals. I heard a few of the staff in the dining area mocking him. "That beard, those sandals, who does he think he is? Jesus Christ?" I looked around at the smirking faces. "After what he has done, as far as I am concerned, he is Jesus Christ," I said.[4]

War zones aren't the only places where human rights are being violated. In some of the world's most ostensibly peaceful venues, human rights are severely restricted. The example of China is perhaps most well understood; even the right to give birth is curtailed there. Would that China's example were unique. Cuba's situation is particularly vivid: an island has become, for all intents and purposes, a prison. Maplecroft's "Human Rights Risk Atlas 2013" lists the ten nations where human rights violations were considered to be most severe:

10. South Sudan

9. Yemen

8. Syria

7. Iraq

6. Myanmar

5. Pakistan

4. Afghanistan

3. Somalia

2. Democratic Republic of the Congo

1. Sudan[5]

There are at least two features of this list that warrant comment. First, while several of the nations on this list are quite familiar (notably Iraq, Afghanistan and Pakistan), most are comparatively unknown. South Sudan is a particularly clear example of this, only having been established as a nation in July 2011. In this light, a great deal of prayerful research is needed in order to understand the needs of the people of this country or the others on this list, and to engage with or establish groups that might be of help.

Second, a couple of nations are notably *not* on this list. North Korea, an entirely insular nation, is infamous for the repression of its citizens. We know well how intolerant this nation can be of any dissent. If this is what things are like in North Korea, what must it be like in these other nations? So also, the population of China is such that the scope of its government's abuses entirely engulfs a list such as this one: so many people are affected that it staggers the mind.

Organizations such as Amnesty International are actively advocating for human rights throughout the world, but they specifically eschew any connection with a particular religion. Should Christians be less concerned about human rights than such secularly oriented groups? Is it even possible for a man, woman, boy or girl to pursue true equality, life, liberty and happiness (human rights affirmed in the U.S. Declaration of Independence) apart from the redeeming gospel of Jesus Christ?

In an address to Wheaton College, John Piper offers a perspective that puts the fight for human rights in perspective:

> I get very tired of people coming to look at staff positions in my church, which is in downtown Minneapolis. We all live in the inner city, and one of the first questions they ask is, "Will my children be safe?" And I want to say, "Would you ask that question tenth and not first?" I'm just tired of hearing that.

I'm tired of American priorities. Whoever said that your children will be safe in the call of God?[6]

If it's dangerous in downtown Minneapolis, it might appear insane to consider involvement in some of the countries where human rights are routinely violated. But this is just the kind of place where Jesus went.

FOR FURTHER REFLECTION

Identify a country that has human rights issues. Begin to pray earnestly for that nation. Become well-informed about its plight. Consider—and take—steps beyond prayer and information that compel you to live by the faith we claim as one that overcomes against all odds.

21

Fight Racism

But let justice roll on like a river,
righteousness like a never-failing stream!

AMOS 5:24

I N THE UNITED STATES, it is often said that Sunday morning is the most racially segregated time of the week. And despite the seismic cultural changes that have taken place since the civil rights movement, despite the rise of interracial marriage, despite the oft-times ridiculous and ubiquitous rhetoric of diversity, little has changed: Sunday mornings are still largely segregated. On the rare occasions where this reality is noted, most Christians simply shrug their shoulders: "Nothing you can do to change that."

This is not a problem for American Christians alone, not by any means. Shortly after the fall of communism in Romania, I was able to preach at a number of churches throughout the country. The faith of Romanian Christians was impressive; I can remember how, since they could not afford hymnals, it was common for the members of the congregations simply to have memorized the hymns. I will never forget being in the home of one very poor family in the city of Iaşi; their family had suffered tremendously under the communist regime, and they only turned on the lights when company came. The daughter in this family, perhaps in her twenties, spoke passionately about how she had risked everything to be baptized; by contrast, we have to coax many converts to consider baptism. The faith I everywhere observed was humbling and inspiring.

But despite the obvious spiritual vitality of these who had suffered so much, racism was nevertheless clearly evident in Romania, and it is a tremendously potent example of just how insidious a thing it can be. Roughly 10 percent of the population of Romania at the time was Hungarian, people who were kept in the country when the borders were originally closed. And the Romanians and the Hungarians did not get along. I preached at two churches in the city of Oradea. The first was full of people who had a Romanian heritage. The second was a Hungarian Baptist church. The two people groups did not intermingle to any noteworthy degree, and the Hungarian Christians were poorer. I could not discern obvious physical differences by which to distinguish Romanians from Hungarians, but the division between them was as clearly palpable as any distinction between blacks and whites in South Africa or at the peak of the civil rights movement in the United States.

There was one thing, though, that the Romanians and the Hungarians could agree upon: they hated the Gypsies. I have never seen poverty like that of a house I walked past somewhere near the city of Gherla, with the possible exception of the worst slums I have seen in India. Perhaps a hundred Gypsies made their home there, and the smell was utterly putrid; mud floors, children unattended outside, and obvious despair within. Not far from an Orthodox church near Iași I saw any number of young Gypsy children who had limbs dismembered or other disfigurements, since such features would make them more successful as beggars. In these children, we see the horrifying end result of racism: discriminating against a group of people condemns them to increasingly desperate conditions, which forces them to accept and even engage in increasingly desperate behavior.

The problem with racism is not American or Romanian or Hungarian but universal. Speaking about the current American reality, Tim Tyson remarks,

> Everyone in this struggle, adversaries and advocates alike, grew up steeped in a poisonous white supremacy that distorted their understandings of history and one another. That history is not distant. Many who marched with Dr. King in Alabama . . . were the grandchildren of slaves. The boy who told me "Daddy and Roger and 'em shot 'em a $n****r$" is barely middle-aged. And the enduring chasm of race is still with us, in some ways wider than ever.[1]

As you read this, you may well be thinking, *I know there's a problem. What can we do about it, though?* There can be a vast gulf between knowledge and wisdom. Knowledge sees the problem. Wisdom sees with understanding, and in this case, the necessity of action is intense. Knowledge says, "Look at that problem!" Wisdom says, "We have a problem," or better, "I have a problem."

As such, stop. Just stop. See racism for what it is, a preference based on an arbitrary distinction. You warm up to people who were brought up near where you were brought up, or who share a common heritage. You are fond of people who share common interests. A New York Yankees fan is unlikely to view a Boston Red Sox fan with natural affection. But their differences, and indeed, the differences between all human beings, are cosmetic. Skin tint. Hair. Nothing but cosmetic appliances to our souls.

Despite this glaring reality, we are unable to frankly acknowledge these issues. Students at Rhode Island College compiled a list of ten reasons why it is so difficult to talk about race:

1. America is in denial about race. Racism is everywhere, yet nobody thinks that they are racist.

2. America only talks about race in times of crisis, the worst times to talk about race. Race is a taboo subject even though it is central to understanding America.

3. America is still a largely segregated society in which we do not know one another.

4. America's inability to define race leads to confusion as to whether race is a biological or sociological phenomenon.

5. There is little common ground where it is safe to talk about race. The deep and unfounded beliefs that are held about the superiority and inferiority of peoples need to be critically discussed.

6. When people talk about race it is often in terms of "winners" and "losers," "victims" and "victimizers," "oppressors" and "oppressed." Those who are privileged by race have no idea why they are privileged, or have no incentive to talk about race or white privilege.

7. Race and non-Western cultures are not taught in schools. Diversity is for everybody, including whites. The dialogue on race in school is often silenced or marginalized instead of being encouraged and protected.

8. Where are our leaders? Who will come forward to be our moderator(s) in a national forum on race?

9. People can't talk about race because they have fears of being labeled racist. This fear comes from being uneducated about race and racism, and perpetuates the cycle of misunderstanding among peoples of different backgrounds.

10. America is unwilling to pay what it would cost to build an equitable society. There is no financial payoff for solving America's race problem, while the true wealth of America lies in its diversity.[2]

Despite this, Carolyn Fluehr-Lobban speaks optimistically about tools that can be leveraged that will lead to "the eventual eradication of racism."[3] But is this realistic?

At its core, racism is a sin issue, and no suite of anthropological tools, no social program, no government initiative, no corporate diversity challenge will do anything other than apply lipstick to the corpse. Only God can shake a man or woman into seeing their own prejudices. Only God can compel us to strive to make a lasting difference in the lives of those we touch. James, Jesus' half-brother, points to inequities that exist between human beings, and he signals something of the urgent nature of the charge to all Christians to be studiously watchful in this regard:

> My brothers, as believers in our glorious Lord Jesus Christ, don't show favoritism. Suppose a man comes into your meeting wearing a gold ring and fine clothes, and a poor man in shabby clothes also comes in. If you show special attention to the man wearing fine clothes and say, "Here's a good seat for you," but say to the poor man, "You stand there" or "Sit on the floor by my feet," have you not discriminated among yourselves and become judges with evil thoughts? . . .
>
> If you really keep the royal law found in Scripture, "Love your neighbor as yourself," you are doing right. But if you show favoritism, you sin and are convicted by the law as lawbreakers. For whoever keeps the whole law and yet stumbles at just one point is guilty of breaking all of it. For he who said, "Do not commit adultery," also said, "Do not murder." If you do not commit adultery but do commit murder, you have become a lawbreaker.
>
> Speak and act as those who are going to be judged by the law that gives freedom, because judgment without mercy will

be shown to anyone who has not been merciful. Mercy triumphs over judgment! (James 2:1-13)

You will note that James makes no mention of racism or prejudice in this passage. But make no mistake, *discrimination* is surely in view. When one discriminates between two human beings, making judgments based only on externals, the "royal law" is violated. *Favoritism* is another dimension of prejudice that James brings out.

If, as you have read this chapter, you have been thinking that racism is not a *church* problem, I would suggest otherwise. As I noted earlier, my youngest son is African American, and I am Hispanic. Over the course of the years, it has become evident that I have not been considered to be a viable candidate for various church positions I have applied for, exclusively because of one of these two facts. (It should be noted that no one should want to go to a church that doesn't want him for reasons associated with ethnicity.) On a recent Sunday, after I made an announcement that a young woman in need would need a place to stay for a couple of weeks, a member of the congregation came up to me and bluntly asked, "Is she white?" It is rare to see such racism so plainly on display. But think about it: this woman, who loved me and my family, who knew that my own son was black, felt no compunction about asking me this. And even with my own minority status, and my own affection for a child of another race, even in that most obvious of instances, my own natural response was to play along: I simply said in response, "Yes." Don't pretend we don't have a problem in our churches—and in our hearts.

FOR FURTHER REFLECTION

Pursue a deeper friendship with one other person or family whose ethnicity differs from your own.

22

Fight Drug and Alcohol Abuse

So if the Son sets you free, you will be free indeed.

JOHN 8:36

I REMEMBER HAVING A CONVERSATION with a younger friend recently. She had been back home to the rural area where she had been brought up and was concerned about her cousin. I asked her three questions:

- Is he very thin?
- Does he look much older than he is?
- What are his teeth like?

These may seem like peculiar questions to ask anyone, much less a bright young spark freshly back from Christmas vacation. But with a real seriousness, she indicated that yes, he is quite thin, yes, he looks much older than he is, and yes, he has lost several teeth already. It was clear that her cousin was addicted to crystal meth.

There were at least two things that may not have been evident to my young friend. First, it's quite possible that her cousin might soon be dead. And second, he has no one who cares. My young friend could not think of a single thing that could be done to help.

It is no challenge to find stories about people who have been rescued from drug or alcohol addictions, or stories of others whose lives have been destroyed by the same. This fact must jar us, because it points to the magnitude of the problem. Drug and alcohol abuse is all around us, present in every neighborhood, available anywhere, a torturous pandemic laying waste to millions upon millions of souls all around the world. All of us, it seems, could point to the wreckage, the carnage of these ills.

But what is a person to do? Think about the magnitude of help this young woman's cousin would require to enjoy real health.

First, he would have to be taken, forcibly or otherwise, to a place where he could overcome the immediate effects of the agonizing withdrawal from meth.

Second, he would need to go through rehab—and not the brief sort: meth addiction is not easily overcome. Relapse is common.

Third, he would need to, through prolonged rehab or through some other means, begin to regain physical health. In time, one would hope, he would obtain clarity of mind.

Then and only then, it seems to me, might he be able to fully comprehend the gospel of Jesus Christ. It's not that truth could not be shared throughout the journey back from the edge, but someone who had helped him through the very difficult steps required to obtain health would surely earn his hearing like no other.

The trouble is obvious: the cost and effort required to help this one soul on the margins of society are unimaginably high. Worse still, the one you would be trying to help would likely resist the help that was offered. Relapse would be even more likely in a case such as this. How could you ever justify the expenditure or effort required to help this one? Couldn't our ministry dollars be better spent?

Despite Christian rhetoric about the infinite value of just one soul, in a case such as this—a very expensive one—there seem to be few Christians willing to put their money where their mouth is, when so much money is likely on the line. There are far more glamorous ministries to be undertaken.

It's all a matter of perspective, and it begins with considering, *How much will I love? How far will I go? What would I be willing to do?* If it was your own child, consider the effort and expense you might be willing to endure. Might you not do everything in your power? Might you not spend even your last dollar, if it would help? David Sheff tells such a story in the gripping tale of his own son's drug and alcohol addiction entitled *Beautiful Boy*. Some might consider his efforts extravagant, but surely, his account is heart-rending. Consider a few of the intimate and personal perspectives he shares:

- "Anyone who has lived through it, or those who are now living through it, knows that caring about an addict is as complex and fraught and debilitating as addiction itself. At my worst, I even resented Nic because an addict, at least when high, has a momentary respite from his suffering. There is no similar relief for parents or children or husbands or wives or others who love them."[1]

- "Nic . . . is smart enough to justify some outrageous behavior with convincing lies, and he is getting better at covering his tracks. When I discover his dishonesty, I'm confounded because I still think that we are close—closer than most fathers and their sons."[2]

- "I leap on every small sign that he might be all right. I think, Maybe. Maybe everything will be fine after all."[3]

- "How often have we been furious with Nic but then have found ourselves disarmed by his kindness and humor? How can both Nics, the loving and considerate and generous one, and the self-obsessed and destructive one, be the same person?"[4]

- "If your child had cancer, the support from your friends and family would flood in. Because of the stigma of addiction, people often keep it quiet. Their friends and family may try to be supportive, but they may also communicate a subtle or unsubtle judgment."[5]

- "The therapist says that parents of kids on drugs often get a form of posttraumatic stress syndrome made worse by the recurring nature of the addiction."[6]

- "We pretend that everything is all right. But we live with a time bomb. It is debilitating to be dependent on another's moods and decisions and actions."[7]

Every story can be considered from more than one perspective, and in this case, it's not only the father who has written a memoir, but the son. Nic Sheff has also described, often in agonizing pain, his own journey through addiction.[8] Consider some of his observations:

- "It's like I'm being held captive my some insatiable monster that will not let me stop. All my values, all my beliefs, everything I care about, they all go away the moment I get high. There is a sort of insanity that takes over. I convince myself and believe very strongly that this time, *this time,* it will be different. I tell myself that, after such a long time clean, these last eighteen months, I can go back to casual use."[9]

- "The truth was, I didn't want to stop. It's not like I enjoyed stealing or hurting my dad, or whatever. I mean, I hated it. But I was so scared of coming off the drugs. It was like this horrible vicious cycle. The more I used, the more I did things I was ashamed of, and the more I had to use so I never had to face that. When I reached a certain point with my drug use, going back seemed like too far a journey."[10]

- "You just wanna be able to do whatever you want, whenever you want. That's all it is."[11]

- "For myself, I've come to discover that holding on to secrets about
  who I am and where I come from is toxic. My secrets will kill me.
  If I don't get honest about my life, I cannot have recovery."[12]

The stories of David and Nic Sheff are the positive ones. All
around the United States, and indeed, all around the world, few
drug addicts and their families have access to the resources that the
Sheffs were able to leverage to help Nic overcome his addictions.
Can you imagine the complexity of helping even one suffering soul,
or the challenge of supporting and encouraging even one family?

Meanwhile, there is a young man in the mountains of West Virginia who is right now doing anything he can think of in order to get
his next fix. There is no one who is trying to intervene, and by the
time you read this, it is altogether likely that he will already be dead.

A ministry to help those who have alcohol and drug addictions
is one that will have peaks and valleys. It will involve a commitment
over the long haul. Quite often, it is those who have been delivered
from their own demons that are most effective in helping others
who are suffering similar ills. But most of all, it requires someone
who will show love to the unlovable.

FOR FURTHER REFLECTION

Groups who seek to help those with drug and alcohol addictions
are easy to find—volunteers, though, are too often scarce as hen's
teeth. Volunteer.

23

Fight for Fair Wages

> *Do not take advantage of a hired man who is*
> *poor and needy, whether he is a brother Israelite*
> *or an alien living in one of your towns. Pay him his*
> *wages each day before sunset, because he is poor*
> *and is counting on it. Otherwise he may cry to the*
> *LORD against you, and you will be guilty of sin.*

DEUTERONOMY 24:14-15

A MERICAN POLITICS ARE BADLY BROKEN. You will hear many Christians passionately identify themselves as either Democrats or Republicans, but neither party's stance aligns completely with Scripture. For example, there is little discussion in Republican circles about social issues other than to point out that lower taxation helps all boats to rise. On the other hand, while many Democrats advocate for social issues of one kind or another, the bureaucratic morass that supports such programs is rarely addressed, even as ever new programs are advocated. For many Christians, meanwhile, it is difficult to see how one can advocate for the rights of all people when the most defenseless people—the unborn—remain at risk. Because of this, some Christians don't vote, ceding their social responsibility to others, or they pick a side and uncritically join the fight.

The question of fair wages is an example. Many American Christians respond to the question of fair wages simply by falling in line with a party affiliation, rather than taking a step back to consider what, if anything Christians should think about how people are paid. Should Christians be advocating for *unfair* wages? Clearly not. But the core issue runs far deeper than a discussion of the minimum wage.

Many years ago, I worked in a small business run by a Christian man. The business was in an expensive area in the northeastern United States, so the cost of living was very high. Although my salary was a little bit above the minimum wage, I had no choice but to live with my parents. And I was fortunate; if I had not had that option, how could I have afforded the essentials of life? Simply put, although I earned a legal wage, I did not earn a *fair* wage.[1]

Christians in the United States routinely benefit from the unfair wages paid to others. The products we buy are cheaper as a result. In a free world economy, however, it is difficult to connect one's purchases with the hardships that others have endured. Even more, refusing to buy products that are made by people earning unfair wages—an impulse commonly praised as socially responsible—may in fact make the immediate situation far worse for the poor, who may lose what little income they are earning as their employers make staff cuts. But it is worth pausing for a moment to consider a couple of specific examples that may help underscore the urgency of fair wages.

Gabriel Thompson provides three vignettes of what it is like to do, as he puts it, "the jobs most Americans won't do."[2] The life of a lettuce cutter, for example, is almost unimaginably difficult; we rarely consider what it's taken for human beings to help us eat healthy (assuming we avoid the bacon bits and high-calorie dressings). Many of us can point to jobs in our own past that may not have been as intense physically as lettuce-picking, but were nevertheless demanding—and low-paying. I myself worked each of five summers in a factory, churning out computer parts (in a job that is now likely done in another part of the world). But consider what Thompson describes from his experience as a lettuce cutter:

> Each morning we complete 10 pallets of lettuce. Each pallet has 40 boxes, and each box about 25 heads of lettuce—which means that our crew cuts and packs 10,000 heads of lettuce before the first break, or nearly 800 heads a person. In a typical day we cut 30,000 heads of lettuce, enough to fill 1,200 boxes. On the longer days—the ones beginning just after sunrise and ending at dusk—we can harvest in excess of 40,000 heads. For a cutter, that means 3,000 heads in a single shift; put two of those long days in a row, and getting out of bed at 5:30 the next morning becomes a true test of willpower.[3]

Thompson goes on to describe another occupation with a tremendously bad reputation: working in a factory that processes chickens. Simply put, there is almost no occupation that would put you at higher physical risk than this. The *Charlotte Observer* explains, "In an industry rife with danger, House of Raeford Farms depicts itself as a safe place to work. Company records suggest relatively few workers are injured each year as they kill, cut and package millions of chickens and turkeys. But an *Observer* investigation shows the N.C. poultry giant has masked the extent of injuries behind its plant walls."[4] The article concludes:

> A year after the accident that shattered his ankle, Guadalupe struggles to walk with crutches and said he is unable to work because of lingering pain.
>
> Four houses down, Ernesto Ramirez, a House of Raeford sanitation worker, said he had blurred vision for three days in 2006 after chlorine splashed into his eyes from a loose hose at work.
>
> Down the road, Guillermo Santiago had the top half of

three fingers sheared off last February when he tried to jimmy loose a hose from a grinding machine. Doctors were able to reattach just one finger.

A native of Vera Cruz, Mexico, Santiago said he's reminded of his accident each time he looks at his hands.

"I'm never going to be the same."[5]

One would think that, the more dangerous an occupation is, the better the pay would be. But Thompson explains, as the pay in his new position in a poultry processing plant is explained to him,

She has several positions that she thinks I would enjoy. All of them pay $8.05 an hour, but if I arrive on time every day, I'll earn $8.80 an hour for the week. After sixty days the base rate will increase to $8.80, with the perfect attendance bonus reaching $9.45. If an employee makes it to the year mark, he will earn $8.95 an hour with a bonus of $9.70. The various numbers can make it seem complicated, but the basic truth is this: You could work at the plant for ten years, without missing a minute of a single shift, and never see your work reach $10 an hour. (The one exception is a job in "live hang and killing," where workers are paid extra because they are in a department that is called *live hang and killing*. Their pay scale maxes out at $10.75 an hour. "We don't have any openings in that," she tells me. Not a problem, I assure her.)[6]

It is difficult to comprehend information such as this. But dangerous occupations are one thing. Barbara Ehrenreich offers some further perspective on the plight of the working poor in her much discussed *Nickel and Dimed: On (Not) Getting by in America.*[7] Like Thompson, she worked in three different entry-level jobs and strikingly conveys the challenges that one faces when he/she has to live on the income produced by working as a waitress or in a nursing home or at Walmart or similar enterprises, when these jobs are your only source of income. Some have maligned Ehrenreich's portrayal as overly pessimistic. One author set about disproving the validity of her concerns, beginning with only $25, working for a moving company and establishing more aggressive goals by which his success could be defined.[8] But here's the problem: young white men can get a job that pays comparatively well. Ehrenreich's perspective is a better reflection of the reality that many women and nonwhites experience every day. Imagine how desperately complicated the problem becomes for single mothers, an ever-increasing demographic in the American landscape. Imagine how desperately complicated the problem becomes for human beings working in so many countries outside of the United States.

The Bible, in point of fact, has a great deal to say about fair wages. As only one such example, consider what the apostle James writes: "Look! The wages you failed to pay the workmen who mowed your fields are crying out against you. The cries of the harvesters have reached the ears of the Lord Almighty. You have lived on earth in luxury and self-indulgence. You have fattened yourselves in the day of slaughter" (James 5:4-5). Surely, he's writing to someone else, isn't he? Photius, writing in the ninth century, observed, "Do not overlook the poor and let not his tattered rags incite you to contempt, but rather let them move you to pity your fellow creatures."[9]

FOR FURTHER REFLECTION

The immediate application of this chapter may appear to be directed to employers. For the rest of us, however, it is worth thinking about how we can improve one person's life. How can we encounter someone who is now unemployed or underemployed, and help them move to a truly self-sustaining lifestyle? Are we willing to not only find such a person, but to stick with him even after he has found his first job?

24

Fight for Health Care Reform

If my people, who are called by my name, will humble themselves
and pray and seek my face and turn from their wicked ways,
then will I hear from heaven and will forgive
their sin and will heal their land.

2 CHRONICLES 7:14

For a moment, imagine that you work for a marketing agency that produces a large pharmaceutical company's commercials. Drug companies have comparatively deep pockets, and so landing their business would be heralded as a tremendous coup. But how would you keep that business? Do you think any drug company would be content with an ad for one of their medicines that simply compared their product's merits to those of other pharmaceuticals, helping the consumer make a free and informed decision? Clearly not. It's about making money, not healing. The other drug companies are doing the same thing, after all.

The impact of the pharmaceutical industry on culture has been profound.

- In 2004 Prozac had been prescribed so much in Great Britain that it was being found at potentially toxic levels in the water.[1]

- It seems quite natural to wonder if eating less and exercising more might be a safer and more effective approach than taking a great many medicines for high blood pressure or similar concerns.[2]

- Drug companies, in the business of making drugs, are not making drugs the world needs because they are not profitable. Melissa Fay Greene and James Orbinski offer some terrifying perspective in this regard:

> Although patent protection, with its accompanying high prices, is always cited as the prerequisite for future drug innovations, patients in poor countries were doubly short-changed. "Even with patents, it is not profitable for companies to produce drugs for diseases that primarily affect the poor," writes Amy Kapczynski in *YaleGlobal*.[3]
>
> With the creation of the lifesaving drugs, and the pulling of at-risk populations in America and Europe back from the brink, the AIDS story slipped off the obituary pages and fell from popular awareness. The wealthy nations lost interest, reported Barton Gellman for the *Washington Post,* "'once they understood they had escaped the worst.' In short, it is a system of 'global medical apartheid.'"[4]
>
> [By contrast,] Dr. Jonas Salk . . . never patented the [polio] vaccine and never became a billionaire. When asked why not, he replied: "There is no patent. Could you patent the sun?"[5]
>
> At the waning of the twentieth century, the major drug-makers were presented with a historic opportunity. Crisis beckoned to them to recast the industry along ethical as well as profitable lines, to bring their medicines to the front lines of humanity's gravest health emergency. Instead, they sued South Africa.[6]

As James Orbinski of Doctors Without Borders observes, "Ninety percent of all death and suffering from infectious diseases occurred in the developing world. As doctors we witnessed our patients dying from diseases like AIDS, TB and sleeping sickness and other tropical diseases because life-saving medicines were too expensive, and sometimes not available at all."[7]

By 1999, HIV/AIDS had become a global catastrophe. Worldwide, 19 million people had already died of the disease, and nearly 3 million more were dying every year. Thirty-three million were infected with the virus, and millions of infections were added to the toll each year. Prevention strategies had been implemented, but the disease continued its relentless march. It moved primarily among poor people and people forced to the margins of society. . . . [N]owhere did it hit as hard as it did in Africa. There, the virus had migrated from the margins to affect the entire population. Teachers, soldiers, civil servants and doctors and other health care professionals all over sub-Saharan Africa were now dying of AIDS. Countries like Botswana, with more than 39 percent of its people infected, were teetering on the verge of collapse. In sub-Saharan Africa, more than half of the people infected were—and still are—women. In 1999, across the continent, 11 million children were orphaned because of AIDS. That same year, new life-saving ARV drugs were being used to treat 400,000 people, 99 percent of whom lived in Europe and North America, where mortality dropped by 70 percent. Less than 1 percent of all ARV drugs were sold in Africa, where two million people died of AIDS every single year.[8]

Most Christians hearing such information feel the need to act, although they might be unsure what, if anything, can be done. But when many Christians hear talk of *health care reform*, they are inflamed with political anger: "Let them get jobs" is a common response.

Health care reform covers a range of issues, including health insurance, universal coverage, the place of fitness and nutrition, infant mortality, abortion, end of life approaches, preventative care, the role of the government in regulation, addiction and even effective heath care strategies for Third World countries. Each and every problem seems intractable. But do the Scriptures call Christians to avoid intractable problems?

Health care reform is not simply an American issue but a human concern. Struggling families in Rwanda, addicted children in Afghanistan and the poor in Guatemala are every bit as important as a struggling family in West Virginia. Think about universal coverage—the aspect of health care that causes the most dispute in the United States. Critics suggest that this creates an unaffordable and impossible financial burden. Rather than argue the point, however, it is easy to find common ground, a credible starting point: most agree that health care is more affordable in many other countries, and that even the health care which is provided in other countries is better than that which is received in the United States under the current system. A better system at a more affordable cost should be everyone's goal. The human benefits would be incalculable. Is this not a windmill worth tilting at?

It is clear that Jesus is making a spiritual point when he says, "It is not the healthy who need a doctor, but the sick" (Matthew 9:12). But the physically ill are not able to hear any spiritual truths with any real profit. As we endeavor to address the spiritual sin that Jesus points to—a recognition of our own insufficiency and weakness—we must learn to connect the very basic issues of human need with the effectiveness of our evangelism. We must bring the love of Christ, who touched and healed even the leper, to a hurting world.

FOR FURTHER REFLECTION

Help one family, somewhere in the world, to be positioned for healthy lives.

25

Teach Financial Responsibility

If there is a poor man among your brothers in any of the towns of the land that the LORD your God is giving you, do not be hardhearted or tightfisted toward your poor brother.

DEUTERONOMY 15:7

FOR MANY YEARS, I HAVE EMPHASIZED this important truth: if the Bible emphasizes something, we should emphasize it. If the Bible does not, we should not. The Bible talks about money often, more often even than such seemingly spiritual topics as prayer.

- "Dishonest money dwindles away, but he who gathers money little by little makes it grow" (Proverbs 13:11).

- "Of what use is money in the hand of a fool, since he has no desire to get wisdom?" (Proverbs 17:16).

- "Whoever loves money never has money enough; whoever loves wealth is never satisfied with his income. This too is meaningless" (Ecclesiastes 5:10).

- "No one can serve two masters. Either he will hate the one and love the other, or he will be devoted to the one and despise the other. You cannot serve both God and Money" (Matthew 6:24).

- "Jesus answered, 'If you want to be perfect, go, sell your possessions and give to the poor, and you will have treasure in heaven. Then come, follow me'" (Matthew 19:21).

- "For the love of money is a root of all kinds of evil. Some people, eager for money, have wandered from the faith and pierced themselves with many griefs. . . . Command those who are rich in this present world not to be arrogant nor to put their hope in wealth, which is so uncertain, but to put their hope in God, who richly provides us with everything for our enjoyment. Command them to do good, to be rich in good deeds, and to be generous and willing to share. In this way they will lay up treasure for themselves as a firm foundation for the coming age, so that they may take hold of the life that is truly life" (1 Timothy 6:10, 17-19).

- "Keep your lives free from the love of money and be content with what you have, because God has said, 'Never will I leave you; never will I forsake you'" (Hebrews 13:5).

This very potent and convicting list of texts—covering a wide array of subjects—is only a small proportion of the biblical material relating to money. By contrast, we hear some Christians talk endlessly about issues that are scantly mentioned in Scripture (for example, limited versus general atonement, or the Rapture). We do well to recognize that the subject of money is of vital importance to God himself, and as a result, it must be important to believers as well.

While we might nod our heads when people remind us how easily "stuff" can take up our time and complicate our lives, what do we actually do about it? When we hear sermons about tithing or giving, how do we respond? Are we eager to be generous? Is this something that gives us pleasure? Do we own things, or are we owned by them? Moreover, how might money management be considered mercy ministry?

Our aim here is not simply to get a handle on our finances so that we are not bound by debt or to live a responsible financial life; it is to live an outward life, one directed at serving others rather than ourselves. With this attitude of humility in view, then, what can we do in this area to effectively teach others about the importance of financial responsibility?

At the outset, recognize this basic fact: we cannot teach others what we ourselves do not do or practice. There have been times in my life when I have made enough money that it became difficult to identify with how hard it can be for some people to make it from day to day, much less from week to week. It is important to remember the days in our lives—if we've ever experienced them—when we had to discriminate between the brand name variations of macaroni and cheese, as opposed to the store brand. So, first and foremost, we need to grasp the mechanics of handling money ourselves. We must have concepts such as mapping out a budget, using a checkbook and avoiding debt well in hand.

The more pressing point is twofold: how do we identify people who need help in this area—notably among the poor—and even more challenging, how can we get them to work with us?

It's not as hard to get started in this domain as you might think. Marketers will tell you that when you have an outstanding product, it is easy to sell. So, for example, while it is often nearly impossible to get poor people involved in evangelistic services, they are often quite open to attending seminars offered near their homes on the subject of money management, budgeting, financial freedom or related concepts—even when such programs are explicitly connected to a church. A long-term relationship, however, is far more effective than a cameo appearance. It is ideal to hold a number of sessions, and to offer ongoing personal check-ins with participants to help review their progress.

Another obvious target audience is children. It is amazing how many children gain little to no experience in dealing with money, or exposure to basic principles in handling money, much less encouragement to be generous. Even worse, many children have active counterexamples as parents or guardians, and come to learn their bad habits from them.

But there is an audience beyond the borders of the United States as well. Financial skills can be taught on short-term mission trips, something worth considering when you think about traveling overseas. Be warned, though: money management is not typically the problem among the very poor; the need to produce greater income is usually the more pressing matter. "Money management is, for the poor, a fundamental and well-understood part of everyday life," reports Daryl Collins in his book *Portfolios of the Poor*. "It is a key factor in determining the level of success that poor households enjoy in improving their own lives. Managing money is not necessarily more important than being healthy or well educated or wealthy, but it is often fundamental to achieving those broader aims."[1]

Many so-called fair-trade groups seem to recognize the importance of trading with indigenous peoples in a way that benefits both the sellers and the producers of goods. Pushpika Freitas grew up with her family in Mumbai, and now runs a fair-trade organization that provides jobs for women in her native land, because she believes that these women "can accomplish a great deal if given the chance."[2] Is it not the case that more Christians can start such fair-trade opportunities for others?

FOR FURTHER REFLECTION

Quite naturally, working with the poor, with one's children or in one's church, or in the creation of a fair-trade group is a logical possible next step. But be creative. How might you help others in this regard?

26

Enter the Political Arena

Then the Pharisees went out and laid plans to trap him in his words.
They sent their disciples to him along with the Herodians.
"Teacher, . . . what is your opinion? Is it right to
pay taxes to Caesar or not?"

But Jesus, knowing their evil intent, said, "You hypocrites, why are
you trying to trap me? Show me the coin used for paying the tax."
They brought him a denarius, and he asked them,
"Whose portrait is this? And whose inscription?"

"Caesar's," they replied.

Then he said to them, "Give to Caesar
what is Caesar's, and to God what is God's."

MATTHEW 22:15-21

DESPITE THE POPULAR APHORISM that we should avoid talking about religion or politics, there are few more popular topics in the United States than to discuss what the current president is doing correctly or incorrectly. Regardless of who holds the office, the prevailing discussion always seems to be centered on what is being done wrong. Beyond this, there are common complaints about what the Senate or House of Representatives is doing; polls consistently seem to indicate a very low level of approval for what is taking place. Similar discussions take place about governors and state legislators and mayors.

For many, this is the political arena. The political arena is actually much larger, however, and potentially more accessible. Abortion (discussed in chapter ten) is illustrative of this point: individuals and local groups have been far more instrumental in changing laws related to abortion than national officeholders.

A starting point is worth considering—one's own attitude to the suffering of others. Although we are at times tempted to believe our own local concerns are pressing and severe (and they may well be), many in the world would gladly exchange their reality for our darkest days.

We Christians talk often of obedience, and of the high place of Scripture in our lives, but our familiarity with Scripture does not always bring about fresh action in the service of others. As believers, we are called upon to consider the needs of others above our own: "Do nothing out of selfish ambition or vain conceit, but in humility consider others better than yourselves. Each of you should look not only to your own interests, but also each to the interests of others" (Philippians 2:3-4).

For some, this is easy and natural. For others, this requires a deliberate and even difficult exercise of the mind and will. Viktor Frankl remarks, "We who lived in concentration camps can remember the men who walked through the huts comforting others, giving away their last piece of bread. They may have been few in number, but they offer sufficient proof that everything can be taken from a man but one thing: the last of the human freedoms—to choose one's attitude in any given set of circumstances, to choose one's own way."[1]

We who seek to align our lives to the call of Scripture must hear such remarks as a challenge and rebuke that motivates us to action in the political arena. In his book *An Imperfect Offering,* James Orbinski quotes a man named Jose: "Even if it is impossible to help the refugees, we must keep trying, and find the truth of what is happening, and we must speak. *Sometimes speaking is the only action that is possible.*"[2] Philippe Bibserson adds, "We are not sure that speaking out saves people but we are certain that silence kills."[3]

Consider the experiences of four others who have been active in the political arena, seeking to make a positive difference in areas we might think of as intractable. Lisbeth Schorr, reflecting on James Rouse's work on transforming the inner city, points to his favorite saying: "Whatever ought to be, can be."

> I remember the first time I encountered Rouse's passion for changing the world. It was 1990, and he had gathered a few of us over dinner in a hotel dining room overlooking the Baltimore harbor to solicit advice on next steps for his work in Baltimore's Sandtown neighborhood. He asked us to join hands as he said grace, and then—his eyes shining—explained his purpose. He was determined to demonstrate that it was possible to transform life at the bottom, in neighborhoods like Sandtown, and that it would cost less to do this than not to do it. He told us that he was filled with horror at the lives people live at the bottom of the American city, and filled with hope that he could show that this need not be.[4]

Rouse succeeded in improving communities not only in Baltimore but elsewhere in Maryland, and even in Boston. His goal was "the transformation of inner-city neighborhoods."[5]

Elevating the status of minority groups—in some cases, people who have been oppressed or underprivileged by virtue of skin color or ethnic origin—is also considered to be an intractable problem, but there are those who, despite the odds, are seeking to make the lives of others better. In his work *Reflections on Community Organi-*

zation Jack Rothman gathers together a varied set of views, ranging from political scientists, psychologists, historians, sociologists and educators. Among the aims presented is the elevation of the stature and status of black Americans. He writes, "A magnificent accomplishment of the Community Action Program was the training of a corps of African Americans (and other minorities) in the arts of politics and community advocacy resulting, for blacks, in a new political class, a constellation of advocacy organizations, a significant body of professionals, and a substantial middle class."[6] Sadly, by contrast, in too many churches, much work in this domain is left undone under this simplistic banner: "We had to get jobs. Let them work."

Community Organizing and Developing by Herbert and Irene Rubin rightly emphasizes that effective community organization is something of a moving target. "The problems and programs designed to deal with them continue to change. Community organizers need to know the details of these programs, the problems they cause, and the opportunities they present and where to look for updated information. Organizers need to help frame the problems so that people can see that problems are shared and that collective solutions are possible and appropriate."[7] The Rubins help underscore the often heavy administrative burden that comes with developing groups that have to coordinate volunteers, raise funds and engage with others—skill sets that can be found and leveraged in our churches.

Jesus himself said, "The poor you will always have with you" (Matthew 26:11), but he did not say, "So you should never help them." On the contrary, in Luke's Gospel, we see that he says simply, "Blessed are you who are poor" (Luke 6:20). Even a casual review of Scripture reveals God's heart of concern for the poor. The resources considered here, and the work which has been undertaken by others, has not been done as a part of any overt Christian group.

But helping other people should not be a political concern alone.
Given the frequent commands in Scripture along these lines, Christians should have far greater motivation to be of help to others.
Some Christians, however, have wrongly used Scripture to abandon
the political landscape, even though Jesus engaged with the political leaders of his day, as did Paul and the other apostles. We fall
short of the calling of God's Word if we neglect this central duty.

FOR FURTHER REFLECTION

Determine which issue you or your church are most passionate about,
an issue that requires significant social change, and set to work. Read
everything you can. Approach the project as you might approach the
most challenging problems in your school or workplace. Real cultural transformation begins with one person's decision.

27

Be Outspoken

*He will take pity on the weak and the needy
and save the needy from death.
He will resue them from oppression and violence
for precious is their blood in his sight.*

PSALM 72:13-14

M ATTHEW 23 IS A LITANY OF JESUS confronting the Pharisees with repeated expressions of "Woe unto you." This is surprising, if you consider how history has dramatically altered our understanding of what it meant to be a Pharisee. In our day, the term *Pharisee*, where it is understood, denotes a pompous pariah, a religious windbag. In Jesus' day, though, to be a Pharisee was to hold a title worthy of reverence, reserved for religious leaders who embodied learning, self-discipline, and piety. When Jesus railed against them, dressing them down as "blind guides" or "hypocrites" or—perhaps most piercingly—as ignorant in the Law, his brazen candor was at once shocking and revealing. It is only because of Jesus' penetrating insights that the people of his day came to recognize the self-aggrandizing position of the Pharisees, who had used religion to their own advantage and to the detriment of others.

To characterize Jesus as outspoken is a chronic understatement. It appeared as if there was constantly on Jesus' mind and on his lips a willingness to speak more plainly than others were accustomed to.[1]

The irony here is the vivid contrast between Jesus and his followers. Christians have become a timid people. There is chronic guilt in place about this, typically surfacing in situations where there has been a reluctance to identify oneself as a Christian at work or to tell someone else about Jesus.

Christian history reveals how it is that the outspoken have served the church. Martin Luther's venomous beat-down of Erasmus, for example, is the stuff of legend: "Your book," he wrote, "struck me as so cheap and paltry that I felt profoundly sorry for you, defiling as you were your very elegant and ingenious style with such trash, and quite disgusted at the utterly unworthy matter that was being conveyed in such rich ornaments of eloquence, like refuse or ordure being carried in gold and silver vases."[2]

It was not just doctrinal matters that raised Luther's ire, but a lack of a true living out of the gospel. In a letter to George Spalatin written from his home in Wittenberg, Luther wrote:

> Everywhere I see things that trouble me, and I fear that we shall soon be deprived of the Word of grace on account of our incredible ingratitude and our contempt for it. Almost all the churches are thinking, "Let us free ourselves from the burden of the poor and send them to Wittenberg." We have daily experience of this sentiment. No one is any longer willing to do good and help the poor. Meanwhile, we pursue our own interests to the point of frenzy.[3]

There are pharisees in our day as well, and our day requires new heralds against the thin religious veneer that covers their whitewashed bones. Whole denominations in Christendom have superficial, token, even fraudulent involvement in missions or outreach. Their view of evangelism and mercy is that "they will come to us."

"Those who see me," the fools and Pharisees will say, "will be drawn to Christ by my life." These modern pharisees profess allegiance to Christ and the Bible, but the real heresy in their camp is to run afoul of their hierarchies or their dusty confessional statements replete with a thousand idiosyncratic nuances.

Exactly how will the marginalized be drawn to Christ if they have to seek us out? In the same way that Jesus was outspoken, so also we must call attention to these sad realities. As such, we must *go to them* in love and compassion without condescension, appealing to the frigid religious among us in no uncertain terms.

The real danger here is a sanctimonious self-righteousness on our own part. As a result, outspokenness must be coupled with humility and prayer. In brokenness, and with real concern, let us nevertheless boldly speak out against Phariseeism in our world.

FOR FURTHER REFLECTION

Prayerfully, and with humility, seek out a difficult conversation that will require you to be bold in your proclamation of the gospel.

28

Go Somewhere No One Else Is Willing to Go

> *But the needy will not always be forgotten,*
> *nor the hope of the afflicted ever perish.*
>
> **PSALM 9:18**

NOT LONG AGO, I HAD THE OPPORTUNITY to spend a few days in Bangalore, India, a leading light in India's newfound prosperity. Because I was there on business, I was staying in a fine hotel with several excellent restaurants in-house and had a driver available to take me back and forth in fulfillment of my duties. The culture shock was nevertheless severe. The legendary traffic in Bangalore is an ever-snarling miasma of fumes, a cacophony of unceasing horns, invented lanes and routes. One's jet lag is not helped by the daily 5 a.m. Muslim chants projected via loudspeakers. And just outside the wall of the hotel was a makeshift settlement of ramshackle shacks.

Move out into less affluent, less well-traveled parts of India, and one encounters the more genuine experience. Atul Gawande, a Stanford and Harvard-trained surgeon, recounts an experience in which he was able to spend two months in India at various hospitals. Happily, life expectancy in India has increased tremendously in recent years, as it has in many parts of the world. Still, the descriptions of the realities of medical treatment that Gawande conveys are disturbing. He writes,

> The Nandad hospital . . . is the lone public hospital serving a district of 1,400 villages like Uti, a population of 2.3 million people. It has five-hundred beds, three main operating rooms, and, I found when I visited, just nine general surgeons. (Imagine Kansas with just nine surgeons.) Its two main buildings are four stories high and made of cement and beige stucco. The surgeons arrive each morning to a crush of several hundred people pressing their way into the outpatient clinics. At least two hundred of them are there for the surgery clinic. The inpatient surgical wards are already full. Calls to consult on patients on other services never seem to cease. And the puzzle to me was: How do they do it? How do the surgeons possibly take care of all the hernias and tumors, the appendicitis cases and kidney stones—and manage to sleep, live, survive themselves?[1]

Gawande's experience helps illustrate the harsh realities of ministries of mercy in such venues. Christian mission work has always been a miserably difficult and selfless venture. To be a Christian missionary today in rural India, for example, requires remarkable selflessness. How much more difficult must it have been for William Carey, when at the end of the eighteenth century, he arrived in India? Similarly, what were conditions like for David Brainerd when he was exposed to the elements among the Native Americans in the wilderness of New England? What was it that compelled Jim Elliott to reach out to the Waodani people of Ecuador? What was it that led such men to such selflessness? And what might compel us to undertake similar acts of heroism on behalf of others? John Piper preached,

I do not appeal to you to screw up your courage and sacrifice for Christ. I appeal to you to renounce all that you have in order to obtain the pearl of pearls. I appeal to you to count all things as rubbish for the surpassing value of standing in the service of the King of Kings. I appeal to you to take off your store-bought rags and to put on the garments of God's ambassadors. I promise you persecutions and privations, but "remember the joy": "Blessed are those who are persecuted for righteousness' sake, for theirs is the kingdom of heaven" (Mt 5:10).[2]

Well then, where should we go? Some short-term Christian "missions" resemble vacations more than ministries; singer Keith Green famously used to talk about his "burden for the Bahamas." Meanwhile, missionaries face pressure to "succeed" from home: I once heard a second-hand account of how a missionary was upbraided because his thirty-five-year-long ministry in the Middle East had yielded only four converts. But this strikes me instead as a life well spent. This missionary had gone where no one else would go. It's simple enough. Where there is war, where there is disease, where there is poverty and suffering, we will find an open field.

FOR FURTHER REFLECTION
Go.

29

Live Unselfishly

*There were no needy persons among them.
For from time to time those who owned lands or
houses sold them, brought the money from the sales
and put it at the apostles' feet, and it was
distributed to anyone as he had need.*

ACTS 4:34

AMERICANS ARE FACEBOOK JUNKIES. All ages. Grandma and Grandpa have come on board. "Let's see, what should we post today? What looks interesting on the newsfeed? How many friends am I up to? Only 507? Surely there's someone I should 'friend' today." Facebook: for many, it's an exercise in narcissism.

Don't get me wrong. I see some good in Facebook. Used thoughtfully, it can help people stay connected. But those photo albums. Don't they seem to be a teensy bit overdone? Hundreds of pictures. Does anybody really need twelve nuanced shots of the same silly pose? This is surely the most photographed generation the world has ever known. And the recording of the minutest details of our lives—would even your very best friend care that you've now cleaned up after dinner and are settling down to watch TV? What conclusions will archaeologists two centuries from now draw about twenty-first-century Americans? That they liked food? As the kids say, it's TMI.

Facebook seems to be an appropriate metaphor for our culture. Facebook allows us to be a star, if only on our own page. Look how cool I am. Look how pretty I am. Look how musical I am. Look how smart I am. Look how religious I am. *It's all about me.*

Though it's disingenuous to generalize broadly about other generations, it does appear that we specialize in narcissism to an unprecedented degree. Our grandparents had a few well-treasured photos, and as a result each one counted. A handful of pictures might actually imprint on the memory indelibly. Less is more.

Psychologist Jean Twenge has written insightfully about Generation Me.[1] Twenge cites one children's book, *The Lovables in the Kingdom of Self-Esteem,* as an example of the self-esteem curriculum that the current generation has been brought up on. The mantra goes like this: children need to feel good about themselves. This is foremost. From preschool on, children are encouraged to love and accept themselves. As is. This is in sharp contrast to the indoctrination of previous generations, who received the clear message that they were largely unsatisfactory and in training. As Twenge puts it, "GenMe has printed step-by-step directions from Yahoo! Maps—and most of the time we don't even need them, since the culture of the self is our hometown. We don't have to join groups or talk of journeys, because we're already there. We don't need to 'polish' the self . . . because we take for granted that it's already shiny. We don't need to look inward; we already know what we will find."[2]

Walk through the aisles of Target, and you are sure to see an extensive collection of princess attire, compliments of Disney. This is available all year round. Our culture encourages little girls to play out the princess fantasy. College freshmen admit to still being gripped by this fantasy. It's no surprise, then, that when it's time to marry, the princess phenomenon lingers. The staging of weddings today will strike anyone who got married twenty years ago. Bridal showers now include an album titled "Our Story." And, oh my, how today's brides *Say Yes to the Dress*. The try-ons. The preparatory tanning. The manicure. Professional makeup application on the morning of. And then the "reveal" of the dress to the groom, all caught of course on camera and quickly posted to Facebook. After an event of this magnitude, the marriage itself must seem anticlimactic.

The tide of narcissism has us in its undertow, from an early age. Coupled with this is the dearth of close personal relationships that Generation Me is able to sustain. Wait—what about those 507 Facebook friends? Does anyone really believe that these are real relationships? Twenge reports that Generation Me reports more loneliness and isolation than people reported in the 1950s. Four times as much.[3] All this self-esteem, and we are feeling emptier than ever.

What will fill us and give us the sense of purpose that a life well lived requires? A look at the early church may provide some inspiration for a life that is conducted according to a different set of values.

All the believers were one in heart and mind. No one claimed that any of his possessions was his own, but they shared everything they had. With great power the apostles continued to testify to the resurrection of the Lord Jesus, and much grace was upon them all. There were no needy persons among them. For from time to time those who owned lands or houses sold them, brought the money from the sales and put it at the apostles' feet, and it was distributed to anyone as he had need. Joseph, a Levite from Cyprus, whom the apostles called Barnabas (which means Son of Encouragement), sold a field he owned and brought the money and put it at the apostles' feet. (Acts 4:32-37)

Early Christians lived *collaboratively*. Perhaps they lived the original "purpose-driven life." They were other-oriented, looking for opportunities to serve their fellow believers. Their lifestyle was simple but revolutionary: they shared what they had. *Therefore, there were no needy persons among them.* No narcissism either. The poet Dante in his *Divine Comedy* describes a similar state as he sketches out a scene in Paradise. He points to a state of love whereby all of the souls are constantly giving and constantly satisfied. We might paraphrase, "The more love, the more love."

There are some signs that today's youth are hungry for purpose. High schoolers are expected to put in a certain number of hours of community service, and many find these hours eye-opening and meaningful. Whether it's helping with Special Olympics, wrapping Christmas presents for a family adopted for the holiday season or painting a deck for an elderly person, service projects help young people see the world through someone else's eyes, attuning them to the needs of others. In the process, the habit of service "takes" with some of them. Often students will describe an experience with Habitat for Humanity or a camp for disabled children or the like as one of the most meaningful experiences of their lives. Some of them are changed forever through these experiences.

It is easy to feel overwhelmed, however; there are so many worthwhile organizations, so many needs. The trick is to pick an effort that we are passionate about and to do something about it. International students whom I teach are prone to be especially focused and purposeful about their career objectives. One who is currently applying to graduate school wishes to become an engineer so that she can return to her homeland and help address traffic problems. She's aware that there are safety implications of traffic jams, that lives are lost when medical care cannot be obtained when it is needed. She has decided to make this area her life's work. It is a narrow and obtainable goal, and I have no doubt that she will do great good. Just as we assiduously work to help our children obtain their wants, we should work to help them find their work. The work they were created for. And in the process, we should make sure that we are doing our own as well.

FOR FURTHER REFLECTION

Whether you are a single person, or a part of a large family, find one other family in your church that you can partner with to identify a service project that your families are passionate about. Make your first such venture something meaningful but achievable. Your goal is to bring about a lifestyle change—one that is collaborative and oriented toward others.

30

Model Compassion

The next day he took out two silver coins and gave them to the innkeeper. "Look after him," he said, "and when I return, I will reimburse you for any extra expense you may have."

LUKE 10:35

FOR THOSE WHO NEED A REFRESHER, Queen Victoria reigned a good long time over Great Britain: sixty-five years, from 1837 to 1902. The Victorian era specialized in what we would now call civic engagement; writers of the day engaged in what was called the Condition of England debate. They reflected on the pressing issues of the day, including economics, feminism, art, religion and science. In many ways, as we think back on the Victorians, we might be struck by this: their problems are our problems.

The Victorian period was a time of great prosperity for some but grinding poverty for others. A great chasm divided the haves from the have-nots. Though the British Empire was at its peak during this period, marginalized populations—factory workers, children, women—were barely eking out a living. There were bread lines in London. Strikes were commonplace, so familiar that writers like Charles Dickens and Elizabeth Gaskell wove them into their novels. People who could not pay their bills were thrown into debtors' prison.

This happened to Dickens's parents; the memory marked him for life. It is no coincidence that the boy who watched his parents suffer from want created *Oliver Twist,* a child who dares to ask for "more." Or that he created Ebenezer Scrooge, a man with a heart of flint.

If we were to conduct a Condition of America debate today, we might find some surprising realities. Although most college students are not well versed on the details of our economy, they know more about economic struggles than their peers of twenty years ago. Students are feeling the pinch of recession, regularly juggling jobs and schoolwork, often renting rather than buying their books or trying to do without them altogether. They say that they've run out of money on their copy card. They ask if they may email their papers. One older student with kids of her own explains that in order to complete her assignments she has to drive around in her truck until she can pick up a cell phone signal.

All of this at a private college, where students have access to financial aid. These are the privileged ones; after all, they have made it to college. Let's think about those who don't. Kids who are in unstable homes, in poor neighborhoods where drugs abound, where shootings are routine, where food is not to be counted on. There's a little boy I have become acquainted with. Thankfully, a family in his neighborhood seems to have taken him in, but I am not at all sure that he gets meals on a regular basis. There are so many just like him. Homework? Well, no. I didn't do it. My dad was arrested last night. There was a drug bust in my neighborhood. A shooting. These kids are a long shot to graduate. They seem bound for low-paying, unskilled labor. They will most likely grow up and produce children whose lives will follow much the same pattern.

Administrators at high-end schools are determined that privileged students become aware both of their privilege and of the needs of others, like my young friend. For example, eighth graders at one private school are taken to Washington, DC, and led through an experiential exercise where they must endure rough living conditions and barter for food. They are regularly asked to contemplate gritty global problems like human trafficking, HIV and child soldiers. They are required to do community service. These are good-faith efforts to help young people develop an outward orientation.

From the time that our children are toddlers, we would do well to remind them that they are not the center of the universe, even though it might very well feel that way to them in their comfortable homes. Notwithstanding the genuine efforts of educators and parents, true compassion is hard to come by. We are surrounded by people with so many needs. It is easy to feel overwhelmed. Our immediate access to images of disaster—we see the devastation in the wake of a tsunami or an earthquake seconds after the event—may actually contribute to desensitization. Children suffering from famine. From malnutrition. From malaria. From disease. The world is filled with needs. Where to start?

Just down the street from my college is a public university. Quite near the city capital, the main drag is home to itinerant street preachers, aspiring musicians, drug addicts, alcoholics, the homeless. There's no way to avoid seeing people who have hit bottom. College students cannot help running into them all. And that's a good thing because college students are at an important juncture in their lives. They are becoming attuned to need; a habit of empathy, latent in many of them, is being awakened.

Social science studies indicate that even infants are capable of experiencing empathy. For example, babies cry when other babies are crying. This empathy seems to ebb and flow over the life cycle, however. Testing for empathy as a dispositional trait, B. K. Bryant did not find significant differences between first and fourth graders.[1] But seventh grade children score higher than younger children. E. H. Erikson concluded that personality traits tend to become integrated only at adolescence.[2] Those of us who routinely deal with adolescents therefore may have opportunity for many teachable moments. If, as studies suggest, adolescents are at a developmental crossroads in relation to their ability to empathize with others, we who are teachers and parents should consider providing experiences that will help move them toward empathy. When these incidents occur, adults should use the moment to help children develop compassionate responses to injustice.

The parable of the Good Samaritan provides a helpful example of what empathy looks like.

On one occasion an expert in the law stood up to test Jesus. "Teacher," he asked, "what must I do to inherit eternal life?"

"What is written in the Law?" he replied. "How do you read it?"

He answered: "'Love the Lord your God with all your heart and with all your soul and with all your strength and with all your mind'; and, 'Love your neighbor as yourself.'"

"You have answered correctly," Jesus replied. "Do this and you will live."

But he wanted to justify himself, so he asked Jesus, "And who is my neighbor?"

In reply Jesus said: "A man was going down from Jerusalem to Jericho, when he fell into the hands of robbers. They stripped him of his clothes, beat him and went away, leaving him half dead. A priest happened to be going down the same road, and when he saw the man, he passed by on the other side. So too, a Levite, when he came to the place and saw him, passed by on the other side. But a Samaritan, as he traveled, came where the man was; and when he saw him, he took pity on him. He went to him and bandaged his wounds, pouring on oil and wine. Then he put the man on his own donkey, took him to an inn and took care of him. The next day he took out two silver coins and gave them to the innkeeper. 'Look after him,' he said, 'and when I return, I will reimburse you for any extra expense you may have.'

"Which of these three do you think was a neighbor to the man who fell into the hands of robbers?"

The expert in the law replied, "The one who had mercy on him."

Jesus told him, "Go and do likewise." (Luke 10:25-37)

The story is particularly notable in the way that Jesus upends local prejudices. The villains in the story are religious leaders. The priest and the Levite, too busy or too indifferent to get involved, pass on the other side. If they stop, they will get off schedule. They may be out of pocket. The injured man is just too much trouble.

The hero of the story, on the other hand, is the Samaritan. A mixed race hated by the Jews, who would travel out of their way in order to avoid an encounter with them, the Samaritans represented people with no status. The kind that lived on the wrong side of town. In this story Jesus is reversing stereotypes and chiding the traditionally religious. He's advocating a responsive life—one that will be inconvenient and potentially expensive.

The expert in the law needed to learn who his neighbor was. Our kids need the same lesson. The small kid who is being bullied. The shy girl who is teased mercilessly. The homeless man who holds up a sign: they are all our neighbors. What will we teach our children? Jesus urged immediate and personal action.

FOR FURTHER REFLECTION

A school context often affords parents and other church members to model compassion. Whether the school setting is public, private, Christian or a group of home-schoolers, it is comparatively easy to galvanize support for a project that helps people in need within the community. Can you organize such a project?

31

Give Money

> So when you give to the needy, do not announce it
> with trumpets, as the hypocrites do in the synagogues and on
> the streets, to be honored by men. I tell you the truth, they have
> received their reward in full. But when you give to the needy,
> do not let your left hand know what your right hand is doing,
> so that your giving may be in secret. Then your Father,
> who sees what is done in secret, will reward you.
>
> MATTHEW 6:2-4

IT IS A COMMON REFRAIN IN SERMONS: don't just send a check, send yourselves. There is no doubt that investing ourselves—tithing our time and talent, for example—is a noble pursuit. But the idea of *philanthropy*, a generous lifestyle regardless of one's means, is a form of giving that should not be impugned as a second-tier activity. It can be as difficult and challenging to give money to a cause as to be personally invested. It may also be that we face personal constraints of one kind or another that may make it difficult to be involved in a ministry personally, while we can nevertheless be involved financially. If you have asked missionaries who have had to raise their own support whether or not their donors were doing second-tier work by giving, you will know how they value each and every dollar that was given.

For the moment, though, reflect on a few verses that are illustrative of an important biblical principle:

- "Jesus sat down opposite the place where the offerings were put and watched the crowd putting their money into the temple treasury. Many rich people threw in large amounts. But a poor widow came and put in two very small copper coins, worth only a fraction of a penny. Calling his disciples to him, Jesus said, 'I tell you the truth, this poor widow has put more into the treasury than all the others. They all gave out of their wealth; but she out of her poverty, put in everything—all she had to live on'" (Mark 12:41-44).

- "Your prayers and gifts to the poor have come up as a memorial offering before God" (Acts 10:4).

- "Macedonia and Achaia were pleased to make a contribution for the poor among the saints in Jerusalem" (Romans 15:26).

- "After an absence of several years, I came to Jerusalem to bring my people gifts for the poor and to present offerings" (Acts 24:17).

- "All they asked was that we should continue to remember the poor, the very thing I was eager to do" (Galatians 2:10).

It is common for preachers to use these verses (and others) to make the point that Christians should be tithers—giving at least 10 percent of their income to the church. In many congregations, such offerings are almost exclusively directed toward two purposes: staff and facilities. Pastors often feel the pressure to help the church meet the budget, to pay their own salaries as well as the other members of the church staff, to pay the rent, to build a new building and so on. Congregations, likewise, are sensitive to the care of the facilities; they want them to look nice, to be receptive to visitors. But it would be a poor sermon that led with "We need a new roof, and we are concerned that the boiler may not last for much longer.

As a result, give generously." Instead, evangelism, missions and outreach are presented as the primary motivators for giving. Quite naturally, Christians want to be a part of groups that are involved in such endeavors, and so their hearts are stirred—even though most churches give only a small proportion of their income to causes beyond their own doors.

We know that Scripture supports the idea that "the worker deserves his wages" (1 Timothy 5:18), but if you'll notice in each of the verses above, two things seem featured: either the poor themselves are involved in the act of giving (e.g., the poor widow giving "all she had to live on"), or the poor are the recipients of such giving. Is it possible that a different approach to how we run a church might be appropriate?

The example of Waterfront Community Church in Schaumburg, Illinois, will strike many as radical. All of the funds taken in by the church via offerings are given away to people in need; the church itself operates so far as possible by minimizing expenses. I remember reading about this congregation back in 2008, and happily, the church is not only still in existence but going strong.[1]

The apostle Paul, himself a man with apparently limited means, nevertheless modeled the kind of giving that was aimed at the needs of others, and urged others to do the same. A line from Paul is often featured in the offering: "God loves a cheerful giver." As we can see in the larger context, however, Paul's concerns are beyond the doors of one's own local congregation.

Remember this: Whoever sows sparingly will also reap sparingly, and whoever sows generously will also reap generously. Each man should give what he has decided in his heart to give, not reluctantly or under compulsion, for God loves a cheerful giver. And God is able to make all grace abound to you, so that in all things at all times, having all that you need, you

will abound in every good work. As it is written: "He has scat-
tered abroad his gifts to the poor; his righteousness endures
forever." Now he who supplies seed to the sower and bread
for food will also supply and increase your store of seed and
will enlarge the harvest of your righteousness. You will be
made rich in every way so that you can be generous on every
occasion, and through us your generosity will result in
thanksgiving to God. (2 Corinthians 9:6-11)

Paul is urging the church at Corinth to take up a collection for
a group of fellow believers they had never met. In turn, he underscores how it is that God himself will bless such generosity.

It is quite often the poor who model generosity best. I have
worked with orphanages overseas, and when you see how the
people in such settings support and care for one another, it is a
most humbling experience. We who have a great deal by contrast
will be hard-pressed to understand what it really means to give all
we have to live on.

It is comparatively easy to give that which we do not prize dearly.
But what do you love most? Imagine a boy about to go to the prom
with the girl of his dreams. Or a mother holding her newborn baby
girl for the very first time. Or a woman who has earned a promotion
after years of hard work and sacrifice. What if the boy with the
prom date had to give up an hour with the girl? Or the mother had
to pass the child to a relative? What if the woman recognized that
someone else was more deserving of the promotion? If you can
identify with any of these situations, then you can perhaps better
understand what generosity could really cost.

Our God has shown us what real generosity looks like. When we
read in Scripture that he gave his one and only son—his dearly
loved, most beloved son (John 3:16)—we marvel with hushed
wonder. We are to give to others in the same way that God has given

to us. It may very well be that we are being called to give in a way that will forever change our churches.

"Generous churches" must not be an oxymoron; we as individuals, as part of the body of Christ, must challenge ourselves to give in a way that ensures that a hurting world is blessed beyond measure. We use words like *grace* and *mercy* all too glibly; we talk about experiencing these realities, but when we ourselves are in despair, we become depressed, wondering why others are not meeting our needs. The Scripture calls us, in giving money, and in giving of ourselves, to live lives of such overflowing generosity that we give not from our excess but from our want. Paul said, "In everything I did, I showed you that by this kind of hard work we must help the weak, remembering the words the Lord Jesus himself said: 'It is more blessed to give than to receive'" (Acts 20:35).

FOR FURTHER REFLECTION

Create a budget. For some, this will be an entirely new exercise. Budgets, by their very existence, cause us to recognize reality, and more, to sacrifice in order to accomplish greater ends. In your budget, learn to be someone who brings grace and mercy to others by means of the financial resources God has given.

32

Show Respect

In everything, do to others what you would have them do to you,
for this sums up the Law and the Prophets.

MATTHEW 7:12

WHEN WE HAVE NEEDS OR DIFFICULTIES of one kind or another, we expect for others to be there for us—or at least, we hope they will be there for us. But in this season of human history we have allowed ourselves to become so busy that it is increasingly difficult to complete everything we want. As a result, it's almost impossible to free up a minute to think about the needs of others. Many are connected with an umbilical cord to their smartphones, so that they can't even go to the bathroom or to sleep without listening for a buzz, beep or whistle. We schedule our lives in such a way that we have to speed from one place to the next; the slightest delay or unexpected ripple can prevent us from completing this day's urgent matters, heaping even more stress on the next day.

With no slack time, we cannot help but be utterly self-centered, utterly self-absorbed. In this very frame of mind, the other day while I was driving to an important meeting, I was under the gun. It was raining, and this had not made my trip either fast or stress-free. It appeared, though, that I was going to make it in the nick of time—if only this traffic light would turn. Out of the corner of my eye, I saw a young man, probably just a bit over twenty years of age. Although it was raining pretty hard, he had on a cotton hoodie, which was soaked through. I remember feeling sorry for him.

To my great surprise, out of all the cars in the line at the traffic light he made a beeline straight to my car, although I was somewhere in the middle of the pack. Mind you, my car does not appear naturally inviting—there are no hubcaps on it, and it's a good six or seven years old. But here he came.

It was raining pretty hard, so I was reluctant to roll down the window, and besides that, I didn't have any cash at all—I almost never carry cash. He made the universal gesture urging me to roll down my window, his hand moving around in an awkward circle, but I couldn't see any point in complying. I had no cash and a meeting to get to. Finally the light turned, and off I went, with the young man drifting off to find someone who would help.

It's quite easy to be objective now and to realize what I should have done. I should have pulled over. I should have taken him into my car and gone with him somewhere to help him at least get warm and dry. It might have been risky, but it's what Jesus surely would have done. We brandish our W.W.J.D. bracelets, but when we actually find ourselves in a moment where we *know* what Jesus would do—but we don't want to do it—we let that moment pass.

Jesus said, "Do to others what you would have them do to you." Well, if I was homeless in a rain-soaked hoodie and I went up to someone's car, I surely would want them to take me home with them and care for me. I'd want them to find me a job. I'd want them to help me get off drugs or alcohol or whatever I had fallen into. I'd want them to love me enough to actually look me in the eye and talk to me, to actually listen to my heart's concerns. It's really very, very easy for me to know what I would want others to do for me. The trouble is, how do I change my own heart to act in that way toward others?

SARCASM

Rather than proceed in a conventional direction, let's consider our words. While many people are eager to learn a new language, I am actively trying to forget one that I have known since my earliest recollections: the language of *sarcasm*.

What we say, and how we say it, quite often frames our overall outlook. The language of the world we live in is quite rightly pessimistic. If, as the culture presupposes (if not explicitly, at least in how we've organized ourselves), there is no God, then there is no worthwhile ultimate reason for hope. If there is no Savior, then it makes perfect sense that we eat and drink, because tomorrow we will just die. If there are no standards, then it makes perfect sense that a man or woman would be consumed with material pursuits rather than take time to care for others. If there is nothing beyond this life, then there is no reason why we should speak anything but negativity to the world around us.

I grew up in the northeastern United States, and there is no doubt that sarcasm was our mother tongue. It was an art form to belittle others, a form of sport, not always mean-spirited but, indeed, sometimes quite harsh. While my conversion to faith in Christ transformed many of the external aspects of my life fairly quickly, it never even occurred to me that my speech should not only move away from sarcasm but toward encouragement, toward positive reinforcement, toward love. In other words, we should *say* to others the things we would want to be spoken to us.

Many of the other chapters in this book are focused on the specific acts that we should all seek to undertake in order to really bring help in a meaningful way to others. Here toward the end of the book, though, it is worth reflecting not only on what we believe and on what we might do, but on who we really are. Consider an intriguing passage along these lines: "Be wise in the way you act toward outsiders; make the most of every opportunity. Let your conversation be always full of grace, seasoned with salt, so that you may know how to answer everyone" (Colossians 4:5-6). Just before writing this, Paul writes about his own proclamation of the mysteries of Jesus Christ; it appears evident, therefore, that Paul in this passage is talking about evangelism—sharing the faith with others. But if we have a consistently sarcastic tone or a negative perspective, how enticing will we be? Paul teaches instead us to speak in such a way that our conversation is "always full of grace."

It's one thing to talk generally about developing a lifestyle of respect for others; it's quite another when we consider people that we have an in-built *disrespect* for. Adulterers. Murderers. Divorcees. Those who are shacking up. People with tattoos. Yankees. Rednecks. Mexicans. Iranians. Pakistanis. Republicans. Democrats. Serial killers. Pedophiles. IRS agents. Muslims. Atheists. Jews. Terrorists. Slow cashiers. Slow drivers. NRA members. Vegans. Carnivores. Everyone has their own secret list.

I can remember working with a company in San Francisco. This was the first time I was working closely with someone who was undergoing a number of surgeries in order to change genders from male to female. I had heard about such surgeries before, of course, but that's quite another thing from seeing someone who is beginning to use a different restroom than they had been using previously, someone you will need to work closely with in order to correct a problem in the database server. Could you develop a relationship with such a person? What kind of person would you find it difficult to establish a relationship with?

Jesus is apparently chided often by the religious leaders for associating with "sinners." As one example, consider Mark 2:13-17:

> Once again Jesus went out beside the lake. A large crowd came
> to him, and he began to teach them. As he walked along, he
> saw Levi son of Alphaeus sitting at the tax collector's booth.

"Follow me," Jesus told him, and Levi got up and followed him.

While Jesus was having dinner at Levi's house, many tax collectors and "sinners" were eating with him and his disciples, for there were many who followed him. When the teachers of the law who were Pharisees saw him eating with the "sinners" and tax collectors, they asked his disciples: "Why does he eat with tax collectors and 'sinners'?"

On hearing this, Jesus said to them, "It is not the healthy who need a doctor, but the sick. I have not come to call the righteous, but sinners."

Are we not only willing to be cordial with people we might not naturally associate with, but even more, to reach out and cross any social or cultural barriers to do so? Will we be people who draw them closer to Christ, or will we push them away?

FOR FURTHER REFLECTION

Reflecting on the major topics of this chapter, consider a three-pronged approach to heightening the level of respect for others in your life:

- Deliberately make time for others (intentionally put slack into your schedule),

- Deliberately work at making your speech and your outlook positive, and

- Deliberately connect with those you have been uncomfortable with in your own life: people you know, but perhaps don't like.

Remember: the goal is not simply to *do* something, but to *be* a certain kind of person.

33

Care for Spiritual Needs

Therefore go and make disciples of all nations, baptizing them in the name of the Father and of the Son and of the Holy Spirit, and teaching them to obey everything I have commanded you. And surely I am with you always, to the very end of the age.

MATTHEW 28:19-20

YOU LIKELY FALL INTO ONE OF TWO CATEGORIES, depending on which church you attend. On the one hand, Matthew 28:19-20 may be a text that is rarely accentuated in your congregation. On the other hand, in many evangelical churches, it is constantly repeated and emphasized. There is rarely a middle ground.

To help meet the physical needs of other people without sharing the wonders of Jesus Christ potentially allows people to survive in this life in a somewhat better condition, while entering the next in an uncertain spiritual condition. On the other hand, sharing the gospel without caring for the whole person often results in a dramatically less effective outcome: the man or woman who feels genuinely loved, valued and appreciated is much more likely to be open to the truths of Scripture. The word *shalom* conveys not simply the idea of *peace*, but a wholeness of well-being, body and soul.

Effective evangelism, sharing the gospel with others, requires bringing the truths of God into contact with the needs of our neighbors. The apostle John urged, "Dear children, let us not love with words or tongue but with actions and in truth" (1 John 3:18). James writes, "If one of you says to him, 'Go, I wish you well; keep warm and well fed,' but does nothing about his physical needs, what good is it? In the same way, faith by itself, if it is not accompanied by action, is dead" (James 2:16-17). While we may see these as potent biblical notions, unless we act, we paint a thin veneer of Christianity over our selfishness.

Here is a tremendous irony: over thirty years I have taught or preached more than ten thousand sermons, Sunday school lessons, Bible studies or classes, and in all that time the most obviously impactful services I have been a part of are in situations such as a women's prison. I will never forget the communion service we conducted; almost all of the women who came forward to participate were in tears, some openly weeping, utterly broken as they reflected on what Christ had done for them. They were meeting with God himself through his Word and through the sacrament. I can remember one woman who remarked that in her twenty-five years in prison, no one had brought communion before. The gospel—Jesus himself—met human need profoundly. By contrast, some of the most eloquent sermons I ever preached (in my opinion, at least) were preached in conventional churches; yawning and disinterest can be common in such settings even under the best of circumstances. Communion services too often have a formal, routine feeling; it is the prelude to the buffet lunch that awaits.

The impact of a hollow Christianity is more far-reaching than might be imagined.[1] Ask any waiter or waitress when they least like to work, and they will uniformly point to Sunday afternoons—when churches let out. It is too often the case that instead of a true tip, they will receive gospel tracts or nothing at all. It is hard to feed your family on gospel tracts. We wonder why people are disaffected by our overtures to come to church when we have failed to connect our actions with our words. As John Perkins observes, "we need the person of Jesus Christ to transform not just the poor but also ourselves."[2]

When do we ever see Jesus or the apostles invite anyone to church? Instead, they sought out those who were hurting, or who were utterly aware of their emptiness: they brought the gospel to men and women in need.

Let's consider candidly one of Christianity's dirty little secrets: *almost all Christians* are terrified of doing evangelism. A frequent picture set before us is that of the Christian on a business trip. He gets on an airplane, and seated next to him is a man or woman: a potential target audience. If he fails to walk through the ABCs of the gospel or the so-called Romans Road with this man or woman, he has failed. What if, however, the goal was instead to simply get to know the person next to him? Is it not possible that this could be the seed for a new relationship? While most people flying on an airplane just want to be left alone and allowed to hide themselves in the music they are listening to, it is at least conceivable for most Christians to think they could say hello, be cordial and look for an opening to build a bridge. How different this is for the recipient than to be viewed as a potential convert, and how much more natural it is for the Christian to simply make some small effort to be loving.

Our conception of a spiritual life is perhaps different than we might imagine, and as a result, the spiritual life we are trying to impart may be a caricature of what Jesus intended. We think of a spiritual life as either personal Bible study and prayer (along with church attendance), or as a set of inward spiritual disciplines. If we look at the life of Jesus, though, his prayer was a natural part of his relationship with the Father, and his life was full of a constantly outbound existence: meeting others in need, and bringing both physical relief and spiritual truth.

We are moribund, though, earth-bound creatures who would readily acknowledge, if we were honest, that "It is not part of the life of a natural man to pray."[3] Neither is it part of the life of a natural man to elevate the concerns of others above his own. Too often, we shrink back from the hardest human encounters, and it is quite often the case that these are the very people who would be most open to spiritual conversations—provided we simply loved them as best we could first.

In Jesus we see the perfect model of the connection between meeting physical with spiritual vitality:

> When he came down from the mountainside, large crowds followed him. A man with leprosy came and knelt before him and said, "Lord, if you are willing, you can make me clean." Jesus reached out his hand and touched the man. "I am willing," he said. "Be clean!" Immediately he was cured of his leprosy. Then Jesus said to him, "See that you don't tell anyone. But go, show yourself to the priest and offer the gift Moses commanded, as a testimony to them." (Matthew 8:3-4)

While we sometimes focus on Jesus' mysterious command not to tell anyone about this, two things in this account are abundantly clear. First, Jesus urges the man to submit to the commands of Scripture (it's worth noting that Jesus himself *is* the gospel). But second, the object of his attention in this passage must be recognized. The social isolation that the leper would have felt is comparable to the fear of AIDS patients when it first broke on the scene in the United States. Jesus, however, didn't just talk to the man, though, he touched him.

All around us, there are hurting people. And all around the world, there are billions of such people, and we have failed them. I have failed them. I regularly fail them. Too often, because of our own fears, and because of our spiritual blindness, we have failed to connect how intimately human need is related to one's openness to the truths of Scripture. When we are able to meet them at their moment of greatest need, we win a hearing. When we speak without addressing how they will obtain that evening's meal, or when we fail to listen when they are in pain, we lose a hearing. So also, when we bring material comfort, but fail to share the glories of our God in Christ, we provide only temporary solace. We must do more.

FOR FURTHER REFLECTION

Transform your prayer life. For many of us, this may mean, if we are being honest, beginning a prayer life that moves beyond our own immediate concerns. Ask God to walk you through the table of contents in this book and show you how your gifts and talents can best be used to touch the lives of others.

Notes

PREFACE

[1]Ben Carson, *Take the Risk* (Grand Rapids: Zondervan, 2008), p. 7.

INTRODUCTION

[1]Harriet Jacobs, *Incidents in the Life of a Slave Girl*, in *Narrative of the Life of Frederick Douglass, an American Slave and Incidents in the Life of a Slave Girl* (New York: Random House, 2000), p. 128.

[2]Clarence Jordan, *The Cotton Patch Version of Luke and Acts* (New York: Association, 1969), p. 47.

[3]James Orbinski, *An Imperfect Offering: Humanitarian Action for the Twenty-First Century* (New York: Walker, 2008), p. 4.

[4]Ibid., p. 7.

[5]Ibid., p. 349.

1 FEED THE HUNGRY

[1]Richard Foster, *Celebration of Discipline* (San Francisco: Harper and Row, 1978), pp. 48-49.

[2]L. Shannon Jung, *Hunger and Happiness* (Minneapolis: Augsburg, 2009), p. 26.

[3]"About the Food Bank for Westchester," accessed October 29, 2013, at www.foodbankforwestchester.org/about_us/about_us.shtml.

[4]Melissa Fay Greene, *There Is No Me Without You* (New York: Bloomsbury, 2006), p. 100.

2 FIGHT FAMINE

[1]"Full Bio: Jeffrey D. Sachs," accessed October 29, 2013, at www.earth.columbia.edu/articles/view/1770.

[2]Jeffrey Sachs, *The End of Poverty* (New York: Penguin, 2005), p. xvii.

[3]Ibid., p. 368.

[4]This view is in stark contrast to activist Bob Geldof: "Something must be done; anything must be done, whether it works or not." Cited in William Easterly, *The White Man's Burden* (New York: Penguin, 2006), p. 17. The issue at hand must be truly *helping people in famine*, not assuaging our own consciences.

[5]Ibid., p. 37.

[6]Paul Polak, *Out of Poverty: What Works When Traditional Approaches Fail* (San Francisco: Berrett-Koehler, 2008), pp. 13-14.

[7]Ibid., 54.

[8]Ibid.

[9]Jeffrey Sachs, *Common Wealth* (New York: Penguin, 2008), p. 6.

[10]Steven J. Lawson, *Famine in the Land* (Chicago: Moody Press, 2003), p. 17, emphasis in the original.

[11]Melissa Fay Greene, *There Is No Me Without You* (New York: Bloomsbury, 2006), p. 57.

3 GIVE DRINK TO THE THIRSTY

[1]Julia Jones, *A Cup of Cold Water* (Leominster, UK: Day One, 2006), p. 57.

[2]See www.allafrica.com for a wide range of stories on water shortages across Africa.

[3]Alexander Carius, Geoffrey Dabelko and Aaron Wolf, "Water, Conflict, and Cooperation," accessed October 30, 2013, at www.wilsoncenter.org/publication/water-conflict-and-cooperation.

[4]Paul Polak, *Out of Poverty: What Works When Traditional Approaches Fail* (San Francisco: Berrett-Koehler, 2008). That same year the organization which Polak founded, International Development Enterprises, also published (along with The Challenge Program on Water and Food, and the International Water Management Institute) a book titled *Multiple Use Water Service Implementation in Nepal and India: Experience and Lessons for Scale-Up*, freely available at www.ideorg.org/OurStory/Publications.aspx (accessed October 30, 2013).

[5]Kevin Salwen and Hannah Salwen, *The Power of Half* (New York: Houghton Mifflin, 2010). While the impulse for her family's actions may be wholly spiritual, their story is told from an almost entirely secular vantage point.

4 CARE FOR THE STRANGER

[1]See for yourself at www.uscis.gov/portal/site/uscis.

[2]See the 2010 results of the diversity lottery at http://travel.state.gov.

[3]A six-article series in the *News and Observer* (Raleigh, North Carolina) highlighted the often crippling injuries sustained in the poultry industry. Many of those employees are immigrants. See also Gabriel Thompson, *Working in the Shadows: A Year of Doing the Jobs [Most] Americans Won't Do* (New York: Nation Books, 2010).

[4]Judith Adler Hellman, *The World of Mexican Migrants* (New York: New Press, 2008), p. 2.

[5]Ibid., p. xxiii.

[6]Aviva Chomsky, *"They Take Our Jobs"* (Boston: Beacon, 2007), p. xxv.

5 HELP THE HOMELESS

[1]That being said, the idleness of the homeless is a stereotype not generally supported by the facts: in New York "79 percent of homeless heads of family had recent work histories and more than half had educational levels, up to college, that made them employable. Most, the study found, had experienced 'destabilizing' events before entering the shelter, most commonly the loss of a job, an eviction or the loss of public assistance benefits." Mireya Navarro, "In New York, Having a Job, or 2, Doesn't Mean Having a Home," *New York Times,* September 17, 2013, accessed February 4, 2014, at www.nytimes.com/2013/09/18/nyregion/in-new-york-having-a-job-or-2-doesnt-mean-having-a-home.html?pagewanted=all&_r=0.

[2]Michelle Kennedy, *Without a Net: Middle Class and Homeless (with Kids) in America* (New York: Viking, 2005).

[3]Jonathan Edwards, *The Life of David Brainerd,* ed. Norman Pettit, vol. 7 of *The Works of Jonathan Edwards,* ed. John E. Smith (New Haven, CT: Yale University Press, 1985), p. 202.

[4]Jennifer Toth, *The Mole People: Life in the Tunnels Beneath New York City* (Chicago: Chicago Review Press, 1993), p. 35.

[5]Consider as a helpful resource John Flowers and Karen Vannoy, *Not Just a One Night Stand: Ministry with the Homeless* (Nashville, TN: Discipleship Ministries, 2010).

6 SUPPLY CLOTHES TO THE NEEDY

[1]See Blake Mycoskie, *Start Something That Matters* (New York: Spiegel and Grau, 2011).

[2]Stacy Edgar, *Global Girlfriends: How One Mom Made It Her Business to Help Women in Poverty Worldwide* (New York: St. Martin's Press, 2011), p. 3.

[3]Any organization is finite and subject to the consequences of the fall, so that even well-intentioned organizations can be criticized for how they pursue the good. Tom's Shoes, as just one example, has been criticized for its "bad aid, good intentions." See for example Daniela Papi, "Tom's Shoes: An Opportunity for 'Bad Aid' to Generate 'Great Aid,'" accessed February 4, 2014, at http://lessonsilearned.org/2011/04/tom%E2%80%99s-shoes-an-opportunity-for-%E2%80%9Cbad-aid%E2%80%9D-to-generate-%E2%80%9Cgreat-aid%E2%80%9D/.

[4]Conrad Boerma, *The Rich, the Poor and the Bible* (Philadelphia: Westminster, 1978), pp. 97-98, emphasis added.

[5]"Prom Charities Come to Your Rescue!" accessed February 4, 2014, at www.kidzworld.com/article/6583-prom-charities-come-to-your-rescue.

7 CARE FOR THE SICK

[1]Thomas Moore, *Care of the Soul* (New York: HarperCollins, 1994), p. 108.

[2]As cited in David Kuhl, *What Dying People Want* (New York: Public Affairs, 2002), p. 108.

[3]Ibid., p. 111.

[4]Ibid.

[5]One example of a ministry to children with HIV/AIDS is the Mother Bear Project (www.motherbearproject.org).

8 PROVIDE DISASTER RELIEF

[1]Nelson Johnson, quoted in Rachel Luft, *Hurricane Katrina: Response and Responsibilities* (Santa Cruz: New Pacific, 2008), p. 65.

[2]Ibid., p. 18.

9 MINISTER TO THE IMPRISONED

[1]James Austin and John Irvin, *It's About Time: America's Imprisonment Binge* (Belmont, CA: Wadsworth, 2001), p. 1.

[2]E. Ann Carson and William J. Sabol, "Prisoners in 2011," *Bureau of Justice Statistics* (December 2012): 8, accessed November 8, 2013, at

http://bjs.gov/content/pub/pdf/p11.pdf.

[3]Paul Street, *The Vicious Circle: Race, Prison, Jobs, and Community in Chicago, Illinois and the Nation* (Chicago: Chicago Urban League, 2002), p. 4. See also Demico Boothe, *Why Are So Many Black Men in Prison* (Memphis, TN: Full Surface Publishing, 2007), and Catherine F. Collins, *The Imprisonment of African American Women* (Jefferson, NC: McFarland and Company, 1997).

[4]James Orbinski, *An Imperfect Offering: Humanitarian Action for the Twenty-First Century* (New York: Walker, 2008), p. 301.

[5]James M. Shopshire, Mark C. Hicks and Richmond Stoglin, eds., *I Was in Prison* (Nashville: General Board of Higher Education and Ministry, 2008), p. 52.

10 EFFECTIVELY OPPOSE ABORTION

[1]For a terrifying dimension of this reality, see Marian V. Liautaud, "Genocide in Shades of Pink," *Christianity Today*, December 28, 2012, accessed November 11, 2013, at www.christianitytoday.com/ct/2012/december/genocide-in-shades-of-pink.html.

[2]Mother Teresa, "Whatsoever You Do," accessed November 11, 2013, at www.priestsforlife.org/brochures/mtspeech.html.

[3]The White House, "Statement by the President on the School Shooting in Newtown, CT," Barack Obama, accessed November 11, 2013, at www.whitehouse.gov/the-press-office/2012/12/14/statement-president-school-shooting-newtown-ct.

12 ADOPT

[1]J. I. Packer, *Knowing God* (Downers Grove, IL: InterVarsity Press, 1973), p. 214.

[2]Ibid., p. 228.

[3]Ibid., p. 201.

[4]Ibid., p. 206.

[5]For example, the adoption of Native American children out of their tribes and into Western cultural settings has been critiqued as an act of "cultural genocide"; see George E. Tinker, *Missionary Conquest* (Minneapolis: Fortress, 1993).

[6]Harold Myra, *Surprised by Children: One Man's Embrace of Fatherhood . . . Again* (Grand Rapids: Zondervan, 2001), p. 71.

[7]Ibid., p. 74.

[8]Ibid., p. 116.

[9]Tom Davis, *Fields of the Fatherless: Discover the Joy of Compassionate Living* (Colorado Springs: David C. Cook, 2008), pp. 37-38.

[10]Ibid., p. 82.

[11]Melissa Fay Greene, *There Is No Me Without You* (New York: Bloomsbury, 2006).

[12]Ibid., p. 20.

[13]Ibid.

[14]Ibid., p. 24.

[15]Ibid., p. 137.

[16]Ibid., p. 144.

[17]Ibid., p. 27.

[18]Ibid., p. 268.

[19]Ibid., p. 384.

13 BECOME A FOSTER PARENT

[1]Alan R. Gruber, *Children in Foster Care: Destitute, Neglected, Betrayed* (New York: Human Sciences, 1978), p. 14.

[2]Judith A. Silver, "Starting Young: Improving Children's Outcomes," in *Young Children and Foster Care,* ed. Judith A. Silver, Trude Haecker and Barbara Amster (Baltimore: Paul H. Brookes, 1999), p. 4.

[3]Margo Orlin, "Motor Development and Disorders in Young Children," in *Young Children and Foster Care,* p. 93.

[4]Barbara Amster, "Speech and Language Development of Young Children in the Child Welfare System," in *Young Children and Foster Care,* pp. 117-18.

[5]Martha Shirk and Gary Stangler, *On Their Own: What Happens to Kids When They Age Out of the Foster Care System* (Cambridge, MA: Basic, 2004), p. 6.

[6]Ibid., p. 7.

[7]Ibid., p. 8.

14 FIGHT CHILD ABUSE

[1]Barbara Lowenthal, *Abuse and Neglect: The Educator's Guide to the Identification and Prevention of Child Maltreatment* (Baltimore, MD: Paul H. Brookes, 2001), p. 5.

[2]Ibid., p. 5.

[3]Cynthia Crosson-Tower, *When Children Are Abused: An Educator's Guide to Intervention* (Boston: Pearson, 2002), p. 5.

[4]Ibid., p. 40.

[5]Kenneth Lau, Kathryn Krase and Richard Morse, *Mandated Reporting of Child Abuse and Neglect: A Practical Guide for Social Workers* (New York: Springer, 2009), pp. 79-83.

[6]Crosson-Tower, *When Children Are Abused*, pp. 62-63.

[7]Ibid., p. 62.

[8]Ibid., p. 160.

[9]Ibid., p. 136.

15 FIGHT PORNOGRAPHY

[1]For a complete bibliography of the works of Jacques Lacan, see The European Graduate School, "Jacques Lacan—Bibliography," www.egs.edu/library/jacques-lacan/bibliography (accessed January 18, 2013).

[2]Laura Mulvey, "Visual Pleasure and Narrative Cinema," *Screen* 16, no. 4 (1975): 6-18.

[3]While this chapter is written primarily with the recognition that most pornography features women with a male audience, men are increasingly objectified by means of pornographic images, and audiences for every kind of pornography is increasingly varied as well.

16 SUPPORT WOMEN'S SHELTERS

[1]Abuse is featured in the Bible. The account of Tamar, who was raped by her half brother Amnon, is shocking even by modern-day standards (see 2 Samuel 13).

[2]See Diane Stelling, *There Is No Fear in Love* (Austin, TX: LangMarc, 2003). A children's author, Stelling tells her story of healing after fifty years of concealing her experience of childhood abuse. She addresses the spiritual implications of abuse in the hopes of helping those who minister to victims.

[3]Kroeger was cited in Helen Kooiman Hosier's *100 Christian Women Who Changed the 20th Century* (Grand Rapids: Revell, 2000).

[4]Karen Thiessen, "Jesus and Women in the Gospel of John," *Direction Journal* 19, no. 2 (Fall 1990): 52-64.

17 CARE FOR WIDOWS

[1]Mary Jane Worden, *Early Widow: A Journal of the First Year* (Downers Grove, IL: InterVarsity Press, 1989), p. 107.

[2]Eugenia Price, *Getting Through the Night* (New York: Dial, 1982), p. 28.

18 CARE FOR THE DISABLED

[1]Community Rehabilitation and Disability Studies, "About CRDS," accessed November 15, 2013, at www.crds.org/about/index.shtml.

[2]Janice McLaughlin, Dan Goodley, Emma Clavering and Pamela Fisher, "Values of Enabling Care and Social Justice," in *Families Raising Disabled Children: Enabling Care and Social Justice* (New York: Palgrave, 2008), p. 184.

[3]Mark Pinsky, "Churches Mustn't Neglect the Disabled," accessed November 25, 2013, at http://usatoday30.usatoday.com/news/opinion/forum/2011-01-10-column10_ST_N.htm.

19 GIVE HOSPICE CARE

[1]Vincent Mor, *Hospice Care Systems: Structure, Process, Costs, and Outcome* (New York: Springer, 1987), p. xii.

[2]Thomas Moore, *The Care of the Soul* (New York: HarperCollins, 1992), p. 168.

20 FIGHT FOR HUMAN RIGHTS

[1]Micah Albert, "Chad: A Country in Crisis," *World Policy Journal* 25 (Fall 2008): 197.

[2]See William Easterly, *The White Man's Burden: Why the West's Efforts to Aid the Rest Have Done So Much Ill and So Little Good* (New York: Oxford University Press, 2006).

[3]James Orbinski, *An Imperfect Offering: Humanitarian Action for the Twenty-First Century* (New York: Walker, 2008), p. 126.

[4]Ibid., p. 243.

[5]Maplecroft, "Human Rights Risk Atlas 2013," accessed December 27, 2013, at http://maplecroft.com/about/news/hrra_2013.html. See also www.huffingtonpost.com/2012/12/13/human-rights-index-2013-maplecroft-human-rights-violations_n_2287960.html#slide=1879312 (accessed December 31, 2012).

[6]John Piper, "Doing Missions When Dying Is Gain," Wheaton, Illinois, October 27, 1996, accessed December 27, 2013, at www.desiringgod.org/resource-library/conference-messages/doing-missions-when-dying-is-gain.

21 FIGHT RACISM

[1]Timothy Tyson, *Blood Done Sign My Name* (New York: Crown, 2004), p. 320.

[2]Carolyn Fluehr-Lobban, *Race and Racism* (Oxford: Altamira Press, 2006), pp. 256-57.

[3]Ibid., p. viii.

22 FIGHT DRUG AND ALCOHOL ABUSE

[1]Dave Sheff, *Beautiful Boy* (New York: Houghton Mifflin, 2008), p. 13.

[2]Ibid., p. 89.

[3]Ibid., p. 91.

[4]Ibid., p. 96.

[5]Ibid., p. 152.

[6]Ibid., p. 228.

[7]Ibid.

[8]Nic Sheff, *Tweak: Growing Up On Methamphetamines* (New York: Atheneum, 2008).

[9]Ibid., p. 6.

[10]Ibid., p. 20.

[11]Ibid., p. 137.

[12]Ibid., p. 322.

23 FIGHT FOR FAIR WAGES

[1]Small business owners are under many pressures—I understand that—but as a Christian, if I ever run a small business, I will either need to pay fair wages to my employees or find another line of work.

[2]Gabriel Thompson, *Working in the Shadows: A Year of Doing the Jobs [Most] Americans Won't Do* (New York: Nation Books, 2010).

[3]Ibid., pp. 33-34.

[4]Kerry Hall, Ames Alexander and Franco Ordonez, "The Cruelest Cuts: The Human Cost of Bringing Poultry to Your Table," June 25, 2010, accessed December 27, 2013, at www.charlotteobserver.com/2008/09/30/223415/the-cruelest-cuts.html.

[5]Ibid.

[6]Thompson, *Working in the Shadows*, p. 110.

[7]Barbara Ehrenreich, *Nickel and Dimed* (New York: Holt, 2001).

[8]Adam Shepherd, *Scratch Beginnings: Me, $25, and the Search for the American Dream* (New York: Collins, 2008).

[9]Susan R. Holman, ed., *Wealth and Poverty in Early Church and Society* (Grand Rapids: Baker Academic, 2008), p. 206.

24 FIGHT FOR HEALTH CARE REFORM

[1]Jeanie Davis, "Prozac in Drinking Water? Likely So," Depression Health Center, August 10, 2004, accessed December 27, 2013, at www .webmd.com/depression/news/20040810/prozac-in-drinking-water-likely-so.

[2]See for example Dean Ornish, *Dr. Dean Ornish's Program for Reversing Heart Disease* (New York: Ivy Books, 1996). Although this text is comparatively dated given the volume of publication that takes place in the field of diet, and although Ornish's ideas have been viewed by some as controversial, it is difficult to explain away how effective a change in diet and an increase in exercise can be in improving health.

[3]Melissa Fay Greene, *There Is No Me Without You* (New York: Bloomsbury, 2006), p. 194.

[4]Ibid., pp. 190-91, 196.

[5]Ibid., p. 203.

[6]Ibid., p. 206.

[7]James Orbinski, *An Imperfect Offering: Humanitarian Action for the Twenty-First Century* (New York: Walker, 2008), p. 351.

[8]Ibid., pp. 352-53.

25 TEACH FINANCIAL RESPONSIBILITY

[1]Daryl Collins et. al., *Portfolios of the Poor* (Princeton, NJ: Princeton University Press, 2009), p. 3.

[2]Marketplace—Handwork of India, "Our Mission," accessed December 27, 2013, at www.marketplaceindia.com/category/172.

26 ENTER THE POLITICAL ARENA

[1]Viktor Frankl, *Man's Search for Meaning* (New York: Simon & Schuster, 1984), p. 86.

[2]James Orbinski, *An Imperfect Offering: Humanitarian Action for the Twenty-First Century* (New York: Walker, 2008), p. 290.

[3]Philippe Bibserson, quoted in ibid., p. 334.

[4]Lisbeth Schorr, *Common Purpose* (New York: Anchor Books, 1997), p. 302.

[5]Ibid.

[6]Jack Rothman, ed., *Reflections on Community Organization* (Itasca, IL: F. E. Peacock, 1999).

[7]Herbert S. Rubin and Irene S. Rubin, *Community Organizing and Development*, 3rd. ed. (Needham Heights, MA: Allyn & Bacon, 2001), p. 22.

27 BE OUTSPOKEN

[1]Of course, Jesus also spoke frequently on the great mysteries of the faith, which seems to have caused some exasperation among his disciples. During his final conversation with them before his crucifixion (John 16:25-30), he told them, "Though I have been speaking figuratively, a time is coming when I will no longer use this kind of language but will tell you plainly about my Father." They responded favorably: "Now you are speaking clearly and without figures of speech. Now we can see that you know all things and that you do not even need to have anyone ask you questions. This makes us believe that you came from God."

[2]Martin Luther, *On the Bondage of the Will*, in *Luther and Erasmus: Free Will and Salvation*, ed. E. Gordon Rupp and Philip S. Watson (Philadelphia: Westminster, 1969), p. 102. Luther's *On the Bondage of the Will* is filled with such castigations against Erasmus.

[3]Theodore G. Tappert, trans., *Luther: Letters of Spiritual Counsel* (Vancouver, BC: Regent College Publishing, 1960), p. 184.

28 GO SOMEWHERE NO ONE ELSE IS WILLING TO GO

[1]Atul Gawande, *Better: A Surgeon's Notes on Performance* (New York: Picador, 2007), p. 235.

[2]John Piper, "Missions: Battle Cry of Christian Hedonism," sermon preached at Bethlehem Baptist Church, Minneapolis, Minnesota, accessed December 30, 2013, at www.soundofgrace.com/piper83/111383m.htm.

29 LIVE UNSELFISHLY

[1]Jean Twenge, *Generation Me: Why Today's Young Americans Are More Confident, Assertive, Entitled—and More Miserable Than Ever Before* (New York: Free Press, 2006).

[2]Ibid., p. 49.

[3]Ibid., p. 107.

30 MODEL COMPASSION

[1]B. K. Bryant, "An Index of Empathy for Children and Adolescents." *Child Development* 53 (1982): 413-25.

[2]E. H. Erikson, *Childhood and Society* (New York: Norton, 1950).

31 GIVE MONEY

[1]See Sophia Tareen, "Spirit of Giving Lasts All Year at New Church," December 28, 2008, accessed December 30, 2013, at www.usatoday.com/news/religion/2008-12-26-church-charity_N.htm. See also the church's website: www.waterfrontcc.com.

33 CARE FOR SPIRITUAL NEEDS

[1]See Richard Stearns, *The Hole in Our Gospel* (Nashville: Thomas Nelson, 2009).

[2]John Perkins, foreword to Steve Corbett and Brian Fikkert, *When Helping Hurts: How to Alleviate Poverty Without Hurting the Poor . . . and Yourself* (Chicago: Moody, 2009), p. 12.

[3]Oswald Chambers, *Devotions for Morning and Evening* (New York: Inspirational, 1994), p. 496.